Just Outside of Hope

1 Pet. 3:15

Just Outside of Hope

Stan Parris

Son, Husband, Dad, Pastor,
Missionary and "Cousin-Brother"

Life lessons learned from growing up

on a small dairy farm "just outside of

Hope," being an All-American football

player and a coach, adjusting to life as

a minister, and experiencing compelling

real-life stories of "prayer walking"

in Venezuela and other countries

Pard Publishing
pardpubs@gmail.com

To contact the author directly, please email him at reddie2write@gmail.com.

ISBN (paperback): 978-1-7378477-0-0
ISBN (ebook): 978-1-7378477-1-7

Editor: Dennis A. Byrd
Cover and book designer: H. K. Stewart
Cover photographs: H. K. Stewart

Printed in the United States of America

This book is printed on archival-quality paper that meets requirements of the American National Standard for Information Sciences, Permanence of Paper, Printed Library Materials, ANSI Z39.48-1984.

To Charlotte.

Without her there would be no me.

Contents

Acknowledgements

This book was just words on a page until I asked my good friend, Dennis "Bubba" Byrd, for help. His years of experience in writing and editing were not the only reason I reached out to him. We have been friends since college days and we have similar Spiritual pilgrimages. I also reached out to him because I trust him, and I knew he would be committed to using his gift-edness for the glory of God. As it turns out, it was not just his much-needed expertise that has been so impressive, but his consistent patience with such an inexperienced writer. Thank you, friend.

A special thanks to the many volunteers who accompanied me on 52 International Missions Trips. Thanks for answering the call, for trusting God, and for understanding the need to be "flexible." To God be the glory, great things He has done.

Foreword

Dennis A. "Bubba" Byrd

Way before iPhones and social media, I got word that my good friend Stan Parris had surrendered to preach the gospel of Jesus Christ. Stan and I, and our wives, had been friends since our college days. We were all Southern Baptists, but none of us were spending much time serving the Lord while attending Henderson State University.

My career after college was newspapering, something that had been in my blood since writing for my high school and hometown newspapers. That means I was naturally curious. Linda and I lived in Wake Village, Texas, in the early '70s and were active members of Rose Hill Baptist Church in Texarkana, Texas, which means we went to Sunday School and worship services on Sunday mornings. Some 30 miles north and a little east, Stan was an assistant coach for the Hope Bobcats and he and Charlotte were active members of First Baptist Church there. We didn't see one another often, but Stan dropped by our house one day in Wake Village. I don't remember the circumstances. I do recall that we discussed how our partying now consisted of attending occasional Sunday School get-togethers and how we no longer were participating in the vices that were part of our college lives. When the news that he was leaving coaching reached me, I immediately called. I asked if what I had heard was true and Stan answered in the affirmative.

"I want to hear all about it," I told him, and Linda and I made plans to visit the Parris household the next evening. I'll never forget how he explained the call from God to become a pastor and preach the gospel.

"He grabbed me right here," Stan said, tugging heart high on the front of his shirt. "The Lord told me this is what I was supposed to do. I didn't question Him." The conversation continued as we learned that he and Charlotte didn't really know much about next steps in their new lives, but that they were listening to God's promptings.

We played a card game, Rook, that evening on Stan and Charlotte's dining table, sort of reliving one of our frequent college pastimes. "I wonder if it's OK for a pastor's wife to play cards?" Charlotte said, almost laughing, as she tossed the Rook cards on the table. "I'm sure we'll learn more about that as we move forward."

Soon after, the Parrises "moved forward" to Fort Worth, Texas, and seminary and we lost touch as we all were busy doing life.

Several years later, we heard Stan and Charlotte were on furlough from the mission field and living in Little Rock before returning to their post in Maracaibo, Venezuela. We made contact and learned that Stan was scheduled to preach at First Baptist Church in Benton, where Linda and I lived. We made plans to attend. At the time, we were members of a different Baptist church, so Stan, my pastor, Robert McDaniel, and I cooked up a plan that would allow us to pick up our friends following the morning service at FBC-Benton, spend the afternoon together, then for Stan to preach at the Sunday night service of Highland Heights Baptist Church before heading back to Little Rock, about 30 miles north.

Our paths have crossed several times over the years, including an opportunity to witness together at the home of a mutual friend, who was dying from leukemia. I've had a few opportunities to hear Stan preach and we talked some about the fact that he was working on a book. "Let me know if I can help," I told him, and a few months later I found myself sitting in front of a computer trying to figure out how to get several bits and pieces of his manuscript into a book format. The editing part was easy by comparison because Stan is an excellent writer.

It was an honor to be the first to read this book and to learn, for the first time, many things I didn't know about Stan and the work he did as a pastor and missionary. Some parts I read through tears. I found his writings filled with emotion and I was impressed with his ability to put the reader right there with him as he gave his testimony to many people around the world. It was a blessing for me to be a very small part of this book and to think back on the many times we shared — some, I realize now, while "just outside of hope."

Introduction

His family was extremely wealthy — one of the wealthiest in his Southeast Asian country. He was a Muslim from a Muslim family, but in his own words, "not a radical Muslim." His family had businesses in several countries, and he was sent to The United Arab Emirates to oversee their business in Dubai. Emir's (not his real name) lifestyle there became more and more immoral. He was drinking heavily and participating in activities that displeased his family, especially considering the family business was suffering because of his neglect.

Unhappy and overwhelmed with disappointment and discouragement, he decided to end his life.

Late one night, a large knife in hand, he walked along an isolated beach until he was certain he was alone. He walked into the ocean about waist deep and prepared to slit his wrists and end it all. As he placed the knife to his wrist, he heard a clear voice behind him saying, "You do not have the right to take a life you did not create."

Thinking he was alone, he turned to see who had spoken those words, but no one was there. He again placed the knife to his wrist and he heard the same voice and the same words: "You do not have the right to take a life you did not create." When the same thing occurred for the third time, he walked out of the ocean and went to a friend's apartment. His friend, also "not a radical Muslim," had stacks of pornographic magazines in his

15

apartment. However, as he glanced at them, he saw one magazine cover entitled, *Who Is Jesus Christ?* His friend denied having ever seen that magazine and asked him to get it out of the apartment. He did. Then, he read the article. That encounter with God was the first step in his becoming a committed follower of Jesus Christ. God literally saved his life and then drew him to salvation through faith in Christ.

Is there such a thing as a hopeless situation? I say, "No!" There are some who may seem to be further from hope than others, but because of the greatness of God, even those who find themselves in the most drastic circumstances or in the depths of darkness are really "just outside of hope." God is never far away, and we are only one Divine encounter away from the hope that can be found in Jesus Christ.

This book is an attempt to tell the stories of how God worked, sometimes miraculously, in the lives of people I have known. Every Christian probably has seen God working in similar ways and has their own "God stories" of lives that have been drastically changed. Certainly, every missionary could write a book with story after story of God's activity in the middle of seemingly hopeless circumstances. The stories here are not isolated evidence of God's grace and power; they are just samples of what God does thousands and thousands of times every hour of every day in every corner of the world.

There was a period in my life when I was far away from God's will. Instead of yielding to God's call upon my life, I ran full speed away from that call and away from His "promptings." It was a miserable existence, but the grace, mercy, forgiveness, and unconditional love of God touched me, changed me, and allowed me to tell His story around the world. I am immensely grateful to God for allowing me to serve in His Kingdom and to see His activity in the lives of many who were "just outside of hope."

CHAPTER 1

Just Outside of Hope

Maybe you have heard of "a place called Hope," a phrase made popular by then-Governor Bill Clinton during his 1992 presidential campaign and election. That's where I was born and raised: Hope, Arkansas. To be precise, I grew up "just outside of Hope" — at least that is the way my dad always described where we lived. Actually, it was three miles from the city limit sign, but "just outside of Hope" has been ingrained in my mind for over 70 years.

I was an only child, had wonderful Christian parents, did not have indoor plumbing until the third grade, remember our first television set, and during the summers, rode my bicycle to town for baseball practice and free Wednesday matinees at the Saenger Theater. I trusted in Jesus Christ as my Savior at age nine, was baptized that summer in Mr. Ross' stock pond, and attended New Hope Missionary Baptist Church faithfully as a youth. I was an average student in high school and an above-average athlete.

I met my wife, Charlotte, in college and we were married at the beginning of our junior year; I was 20, she was 19. In our mid-20s we answered God's call to ministry. We served churches in four states, served as missionaries in two countries, and led ministry teams to several countries.

Here we are, 50 years later, with three adult children, five grandchildren, one dog, and stories that need to be told. They are stories of God's activity among people ... people, who for many different reasons and various circumstances, found themselves "just outside of hope."

CHAPTER 2

Understanding Hope

"The Christian hope is not simply a trembling, hesitant hope that perhaps the promises of God may be true. It is the confident expectation that they cannot be anything else than true." (The Daily Study Bible Series: New Testament Words by William Barclay)

The Christian hope is based on the promises of God. Without those promises, we have nothing upon which to place our hope. Our English word "hope" implies an expectation of something desired and not yet attained ... "I certainly hope our team wins." The Greek word, *elpis*, implies a favorable and confident expectation. The Apostle Paul uses this word in Romans 8:24 to describe the hope of eternal salvation. *"But if we hope for what we do not see, with perseverance (cheerful endurance) we wait eagerly for it." (New American Standard Bible — NASB)*

The opposite of hope is despair. This Greek word, *exaporeo*, means "to be utterly without a way; no way through and no way out." Christian hope says there is always a way through and always a way out of life's experiences and circumstances. The promises of God remind us that we can and should always have a confident and favorable expectation that God is always at work for our good.

One of my favorite preachers of the last century, G. Campbell Morgan, states it this way: "Hope comes to its brightest shining in the presence of the deepest darkness." The bad news is that this life is full of disruptions designed to produce despair. We will never be able to avoid all of them. But as Morgan says, "If there is no danger of despair, there is no possibility or necessity for hope." The good news is that during and after the disruption, God's enabling grace is on the way and we can eagerly and confidently expect it at any moment. In fact, it rushes in.

I know these are just words, and I know that some who are reading this are in terrible pain. It may be that there is no end in sight, but just because an answer is not in sight does not mean it does not exist. I really like these words to the song, "Haven't Seen It Yet," by Danny Gokey:

Have you been praying, and you still have no answers?
Have you been pouring out your heart for so many years?
Have you been hoping that things would have changed by now?
Have you cried all the faith you have through so many tears?
Don't forget the things that He has done before
And remember He can do it all once more

It's like the brightest sunrise
Waiting on the other side of the darkest night
Don't ever lose hope, hold on and believe
Maybe you just haven't seen it, just haven't seen it yet
You're closer than you think you are
Only moments from the break of dawn
All His promises are just up ahead
Maybe you just haven't seen it, just haven't seen it yet ...

He had the solution before you had the problem
He sees the best in you when you feel at your worst
So, in the questioning don't ever doubt His love for you
'Cause it's only in His love that you'll find a breakthrough ...

He is moving with a love so deep
Hallelujah for the victory
Good things are coming even when we can't see

We can't see it yet, but we believe that
He is moving with a love so deep
Hallelujah for the victory ...

It is always true that, "You're closer than you think you are ..."

Several years ago, my hometown of Hope, Arkansas, extended its city limits to accommodate new businesses closer to the Interstate. My old home place has not moved; it is still "just outside of Hope," but Hope has moved closer. That is what Biblical hope does. You may be "just outside of hope," but "you're closer than you think you are." Do not lose hope.

CHAPTER 3

Olen and Betty Parris

My parents were two of the finest people I have ever known. Neither of them graduated from high school, but both were wise with "a kind of sanctified common sense" that resulted in great life skills. Dad completed the tenth grade. Mother dropped out during the eighth grade when her mom died. At the age of 13, she became responsible for the cooking, cleaning, and caring of her father, three brothers, and little sister. She was the hardest-working woman I have ever known. She was tall, strong, and reserved. My dad also was strong and hard working and never allowed the fact that he had polio as a baby interfere with providing for his family. He walked with a noticeable limp and his bad foot was noticeably swollen every night after work. He would soak it in a pan of hot water and Epsom salt. As tired as he was and as badly as his foot hurt, he was always available to hit a few grounders before supper to improve my baseball skills. He was much more the "people person" than Mother. He could talk to anyone, was very kind, loved to laugh, and was extremely sensitive and tender-hearted.

As I thought about accurately describing their character qualities, the following devotional from *Bible in One Year with Nicky Gumbel* appeared in my daily reading:

"As we have seen, knowledge is horizontal. But wisdom is vertical. It comes down from above. You will grow in wisdom as you learn, reflect, and live in relationship with God. We all desperately need wisdom. In the Old Testament there are several books of 'Wisdom': Proverbs, Job, Ecclesiastes, and Song of Songs. In addition, sprinkled throughout the Bible are various writings, which might loosely be described as 'Wisdom Literature,' dealing with such diverse areas as the power of the tongue, the blessings of faithfulness, the dangers of adultery, the hazards of strong drink, the inequalities of life, the sufferings of the righteous, the skill of leadership and the art of parenting. This wisdom is a kind of sanctified common sense. It leads to greater self-understanding. It gives us the ability to cope in life and to steer through and master its challenges. It is the sort of legacy good parents want to hand on to their children. Ultimately, wisdom is found in Jesus Christ, who is the 'wisdom of God' (1 Corinthians 1:24)."

Proverbs 9:10 — "The fear of the Lord is the beginning of wisdom, and the knowledge of The Holy One is understanding."

Proverbs 8:13 — "The fear of the Lord is to hate evil, pride and arrogance and the evil way and the perverted mouth, I hate."

Proverbs 8:17 — "I love those who love me; and those who diligently seek me will find me."

James 3:17— "But the wisdom from above is first pure, then peaceable, gentle, reasonable, full of mercy and good fruits, un-wavering, without hypocrisy."

Olen and Betty Parris had "a sanctified common sense" that came from God and was rooted in their reverence and respect for God. It was this God-fearing quality that enabled them to steer through and master some difficult challenges in life. There were a few times when my parents found themselves "outside of hope." There are billions of people in the world who do not even know that hope exists (that's right, billions); that was certainly not true of my parents. It does not mean that they had lost hope or that hope had been extinguished. It means the circumstances of life can thrust us into situations where hope is blurred and seems to fade. It is during those situations that the fruit of our relationship with God enables us to focus clearly on what we know to be true about God. We do not have to understand clearly if we understand God.

My parents gave birth to Kenneth Wayne Parris on November 1, 1936. He died of leukemia just before his sixth birthday. Everything I know about him indicates that he was bright, extremely insightful, and extremely spiritual. My parents very rarely talked about him in my presence. The only pictures of him were kept stored away in a footlocker with his shoes and his red overalls. His illness was short-lived, and his death came quickly. He witnessed to his doctor and his nurses saying, "if you're going to heaven with me, you need to be ready and get packed."

One family member once said to me that he had never heard a child pray like Kenneth. I think it would be safe to say that in those grieving moments surrounding his death, my parents found themselves "just outside of hope." They moved away from the small community in rural Arkansas where they were living and where my mother had been born. Actually, they moved far away … to Arizona. I do not know very much about their time there. I know that mom worked in a prisoner of war camp where German prisoners were detained. Dad drove a gasoline truck and at that time, he still used crutches to walk. I am not sure about the time frame, but when I was born in May of 1949, they had moved to Hope, Arkansas, bought a four-room house and 80 acres. Seven years had passed since the death of their son. I never asked them, but later in my adult life I secretly wondered if they had struggled with the decision to have another child after the pain of Kenneth's death. After both Mom and Dad had died, I mentioned this to an older cousin and his response confirmed my suspicion; without ever making eye contact he said, "Well, you weren't planned." Unplanned, but not unwanted, and never unloved. You could place that on my tombstone.

As far as I know, my parents never wavered in their faith, trust, and dependence on God. They never stopped going to church. My dad never stopped reading the Bible. My mother never stopped being an incredible mother. When you are "just outside of hope," it can make you or break you. I do not know exactly how they made it through that experience, but it did not break them. As a result of that experience, they became very gifted at what I would describe as grief ministry.

Some of my earliest memories are of going with my father to visit those who were hurting or grieving. He would go to the hospital to check on someone, but would visit everyone. I have stood silently at a distance and watched him cry with hurting parents. He was gifted at encouragement. Even as a child I could tell that the people whom he visited were glad to see him. They knew he was sincere in his concern for them, and they knew that he understood. He had been there … and he and Mom had found and regained hope.

My dad died in 1991 just a few months short of his 80th birthday. When I cleaned out his closet I just could not part with his Sunday suits. He loved to dress up for church. Mother always made sure that he "looked nice." I kept his suits in my closet for a long time. One morning I received a phone call from a local funeral home asking me if I could meet with a young couple whose infant son had died. In addition to the grief of losing their child, the father was overwhelmed with the fact that he did not own a suit to wear to his son's funeral. I told him that I had one that would fit him perfectly, and it did. Even from heaven, my dad's grief ministry continued to help someone who was "just outside of hope."

CHAPTER 4

Betty Lou Ellis Parris

(October 28, 1915–January 24, 1984)

Mother was the fifth of six children born to Robert Gordon Ellis and Lola Purtle Ellis. The Purtle and Ellis families had traveled together from Georgia before the Civil War and settled in the Bluff Springs community, located in rural Southwest Arkansas. When Mother was 13 years old, her mother, Lola, died from an infection caused by an untreated wound. She dropped out of the eighth grade to become the "woman of the house." Her older sister was already married and her father and three older brothers depended on her to keep the house running and take care of her eight-year-old sister. She taught herself to cook and if she was not convinced it was good, she would throw it out and start over again.

The time was the late 1920's and mother had a recipe box full of her personal depression-era recipes. She was well known for her country cooking and anyone who ever sat at her table will agree that she was an excellent cook.

Until I was old enough to go to school, my parents had a dairy. In those days, the cows were milked by hand; there were no automated milking machines. The cow's milk would be poured from buckets into 10-gallon milk cans and when full, those cans would be placed into a large box-like metal cooler. The cans would remain in the cooler until the milk truck came to pick them up. My parents would get up at 4:30 each morning to milk the cows before leaving for work. They would come home after work and milk them again. It was a lot of hard work, but Mother worked hard her entire life.

When I was in the third grade, we built a new house. The old four-room house with the "dog trot porch" was torn down and much of the lumber was used in the new construction. I was excited because I was going to have my own bedroom. I had always slept in the same bedroom with my parents because the other bedroom had no heat. On rare occasions, one of my friends or cousins would spend the night and we would sleep in that bedroom. Mother would pack us in with so many quilts it was almost impossible to turn over. One of my friends commented to Mother that he "felt like a pack mule." While the new house was being built, we stayed with my dad's parents, who also lived in a four-room house, but they did have an indoor bathroom.

It was during this time that Mother was diagnosed with cancer. She was sent to the hospital in Texarkana, 32 miles away, to receive treatments. I had no idea why she was in the hospital. My dad chose not to tell me about the cancer or how serious it was. I only knew that he would leave directly from work and drive to the hospital to be with Mother. She remained hospitalized for a month and received 30 radiation treatments. They protected me from all that was going on during those stressful days. It says a lot about their character and their parenting skills that I never felt afraid or anxious during that time. Years later, Dad told me he had explained the situation to my third-grade teacher and asked her to "make sure I was doing okay."

Until I was an adult, I had never thought about the fact that my mother had lost her mother at age 13, dropped out of school to take on the responsibility of managing a home, lived through the Depression, buried a son, moved away from her home place, dealt with an unplanned pregnancy, gave birth to a second child, and survived cancer and the brutal treatments by the time she was 42 years old. My parents had been through a lot of "just outside of hope" situations in their first 22 years of marriage. By example, they were teaching me about God's faithfulness and to never lose hope. Mother's cancer would reappear 26 years later and we would all find ourselves "just outside of hope."

CHAPTER 5

Rural Route 4, Box 304

Growing up, we lived on Melrose Lane, just outside of Hope, but our mailing address was Rural Route 4, Box 304, Hope, Arkansas. Ours was the first house after you turned onto the dirt road that ran alongside Long's Gulf Station and Grocery Store. When I say dirt road, think dust, red dust, especially during the hot, dry months of summer.

Being an only child and living in the country, I became highly creative at making up games and using my imagination. When I was 4, Mother nailed a basketball goal at just the right height onto the large shade tree in front of our house. I would spend hours shooting baskets, making up names for imaginary players, and competing in tournaments. Each player had a name and position on the "court" and when I shot from that position, in my mind I was that person. I used the unique shooting style I had assigned to him. I even learned to shoot left-handed when I was Calhoun on the Guernsey team. I did the same thing when I switched to baseball. I would bounce the baseball off the dairy barn, scoop it up and throw it to first base, then stretch to catch it as it rebounded off the dairy barn wall. After breaking several brick tiles in the wall, Dad insisted that I switch to a rubber ball, but the games continued. Hours and hours of make-believe games, made up names, and somehow the team I played for always won. Always.

I mentioned Long's Grocery Store. My parents often sent me on the 100-yard trip on my bicycle to get milk and bread.

Mom always bought groceries in town on Friday afternoon when she got paid, but we were always running out of something. So, I would ride my bike down the red dirt road, pick up the milk and bread, and ask Mrs. Long to "charge it." She would write it down on a small tablet; each family on Melrose Lane had their own tablet. She would place the Borden milk in one small brown paper bag and the short loaf of Holsum bread in another. There is a real art to rolling and wrapping the top of a paper bag around a handlebar grip and riding your bicycle without wrecking or smashing the bread. I was a master at it.

It was a Gulf "filling station" as well as a grocery store. It was also a kind of gathering place for older men who loved to talk about fox hunting. Mrs. Long was always behind the wooden counter, but most of the time Mr. Long would be sitting with the men in the small circle of chairs just behind the Coke box. I can still visualize that store and I can remember standing in front of the candy counter peering through the glass, wondering what Mother would do if I bought a Payday and asked Mrs. Long to put it on the tab. I did test the limits one day and charged 25 cents worth of candy. It seemed strange to me that Mrs. Long did not write it down. Within 15 minutes, I was back in the store returning the candy. Mrs. Long just smiled. She never said a word and I never tried that again.

Mr. Lamb was one of the older men who was always seated in the chairs, sharing stories. He lived by himself just up the road from us in a small frame house. One summer day, there was a knock on our back door. No one ever came to our back door, but when Mother went to the door, there stood Mr. Lamb. I was only eight or nine years old, but I have never forgotten the frightened look on his face. He was lost. He had gotten confused as he walked up Melrose Lane and somehow had walked into the woods behind our house. He was so frightened that he did not recognize my mother and he just kept repeating the phrase,

"Help me!" Mother brought him into the house, sat him down at the kitchen table, and gave him a glass of water. He calmed down and eventually we watched him as he walked safely up the road to his house. What I have never forgotten about that event was the look in Mr. Lamb's eyes. He truly was, in that moment, lost. I saw panic, fear, uncertainty and hopelessness. It was a look of what it means to be "just outside of hope." He knew where he lived. He knew how to get home, but he found himself overwhelmed by circumstances and a situation that caused him to forget what he knew. He was within sight of his home, but he could not see it.

I believe there are times in all of our lives when we, too, are "just outside of hope." To keep from being lost, we must keep hope in sight without letting circumstances or the situation in which we find ourselves affect our vision.

CHAPTER 6

Only Child Syndrome

"Only child syndrome" refers to the *theory* that children who do not have siblings are more likely to grow into maladjusted adults. The theory is believed to have its roots in the work of Granville Stanley Hall, a psychologist who presented his only child syndrome theory in 1896. Hall believed that only children are more likely to have problems forming relationships and functioning socially, and that they may even intentionally distance themselves from others out of a sense of superiority. Hall believed only children are more likely to be eccentric, unpopular, selfish loners who may not achieve as well as children who grew up with siblings.

Other experts believe, however, that only children are at no disadvantage socially, and, while they may form closer relationships with their parents, that often translates to higher levels of success in life, rather than higher levels of maladjustment. Some psychologists and historians point out that society has long stigmatized parents of only children, out of a belief that the refusal to give a child siblings could be harmful to the child.

So, depending on which "theory" one believes, I am either eccentric with a sense of superiority or I am successful and well-adjusted. I will leave that determination up to my family and close friends, but allow me to make the case for somewhere in between.

From 1998-2008, I was privileged to serve on the staff of Immanuel Baptist Church in Little Rock, Arkansas. As the

31

Missions Pastor, I had the responsibility of forming partnerships with Christian friends all over the world, who were meeting human needs, establishing churches, and leading people to believe in and trust in Jesus as the Lord of their lives.

One of those partnerships took a group of us to a Muslim nation that had been greatly impacted by the tsunami in 2004. While ministering in one of the communities, I was introduced to the term, "cousin-brother." I never quite figured out exactly to which family member the term referred in that culture, but I immediately adopted the term to refer to some members of my family. Although I am an only child, I have never really felt like an only child because of my close relationship with my first cousins. Joe Don, Tommy Lee, Brenda Sue, and Jimmy Harold were like my brothers and sister. I always thought of them as more than cousins, but I never had exactly the correct way to express how I felt about them until … "cousin-brothers." Perfect.

I have wonderful memories of family gatherings, attending church together, and spending summers together at our grandparents' house. Our parents had jobs so Mama and Papa Parris would take care of us on weekdays. Joe was born in 1943, Jim in 1944, Tom and Brenda in 1946, and I came along in 1949. Doing the math shows I was the baby. I am not sure what being a real baby brother is like, but being the baby "cousin-brother" had a positive impact on my life. First of all, spending so much time with them pretty much erased Hall's theory "that only children are more likely to have problems forming relationships and functioning socially and that they may even intentionally distance themselves from others out of a sense of superiority." In our grandparents' four-room house it was impossible to "distance yourself" from anybody. We did everything together. All-day Monopoly games, backyard baseball games, 3 p.m. snack time in the shade of the backyard, and wonderful meals as we all squeezed around the kitchen table.

Mama Parris was famous for cornbread and sun tea. She was also known to cut a persimmon switch and apply it to our behinds. Jim and I seemed to be the most frequent recipients of these "switchings," probably because we most frequently deserved them. Meals were always preceded with Papa Parris' familiar prayer, "Make us thankful for these and all our many other blessings." Any misbehaving around the table would result in Papa Parris sending someone to sit in the corner of their bedroom underneath the pressed oak shelf clock that chimed every half hour. The peaceful sound of that clock was always a reminder of family and a reassurance of safety, unless, of course, you were sitting under it.

One of my favorite memories is climbing the oak tree next to the barn. There was room for all five of us in that tree. Of course, Brenda and I could not climb as high, but up high in the tree there were large limbs that forked and made a perfect seating area. One limb even had three strong branches, which allowed someone to sit and recline. That was always Joe's limb, but when he was old enough to have a summer job, we all moved up a limb. I could not wait until I was old enough to sit in that triple-branch reclining spot, but when that day came, I was in the tree by myself. It was no fun with nobody seeing me there.

Also, that feeling of superiority that an only child presumably develops … suffice to say that my cousin-brothers always kept me in my place. They were not mean about it, but neither were they overflowing with mercy. I had to keep up to their pace and if I was going to participate with them, being the youngest was never an acceptable excuse. When I was old enough to hit a home run in the backyard playing field, the game was moved to the back pasture, a much larger field. When we played what we called "choosing sides and throwing hickory nuts (pronounced 'hickernuts') at each other," I could not cry when Joe caught me in the eye with one of his fastballs. They were easier with Brenda, but not with me.

One Christmas, one of my cherished gifts was a pair of boxing gloves. My cousin-brother, Jim, offered to give me a boxing lesson. The fact that he was twelve and I was seven did not matter, and by the time my mother walked into the room my nose was bleeding and a black eye was in the making. So, I learned an important lesson early in life: it hurts to get hit in the face. My mother also gave Jim a lesson that day.

I mentioned earlier that I had above-average athletic abilities. There are two reasons for this: one, God gave me those abilities, and two, my cousin-brothers made me play at their level or I could not play at all. I was one of the youngest players in Little League baseball at age seven. I was competing against 10-12-year olds. We were playing against Jim's team one summer night and I was hit by the pitcher. He was a big boy, he threw hard, and the ball hit me on the hand. I was fighting back tears as I ran to first base. Jim was the second baseman and ran over to me as I stood on the base, leaned down, and said, "You'd better not cry." and I did not.

As we grew older, we were not together as often, but we still were together at church and family gatherings. Our church played a vital role in all our lives. Our grandfathers were deacons; our families were core members; Brenda played the piano, and she played it brilliantly; Tom, Brenda, and I were baptized on the same day in the same pond. The teachings we heard and the testimonies we saw prepared all of us for situations when we would find ourselves "just outside of hope."

Jim and his mother, Aunt Toe (her name was Florine, but Kenneth, my brother, could not say, Flo) moved to Arizona where she had a teaching job. Jim's father survived World War II, returned home, and was killed at a railroad crossing when Jim was three years old. Aunt Toe never remarried, and Jim grew up without a dad, but he chose to embrace the teachings and testimonies of his childhood. I am sure there were plenty of moments when the two of them had reason for despair and discouragement, but they never lost sight of hope. Being an only child, too, Jim was quick to adapt my "cousin-brother" concept.

Joe, Tom, and Brenda lost their dad to cancer in 1965. Uncle Lee was my dad's younger brother and they were remarkably close, even for brothers. Uncle Lee was only 50 years old. It was one of those "just outside of hope" experiences for them. My cousin-sister, Brenda, died in 2001. She had lived for years with neuropathy and had endured excruciating pain; however, she continued to play the piano and Gospel music was her specialty. Tom served three tours in Vietnam and more than any of us had endured situations in which he found himself "just outside of hope." But he never lost hope, and like the rest of us, his faith in God provided direction and Tom followed in obedience.

Joe Don was the leader of our clan. He was the first to go to college, first to get married, and first to have children. In many ways, he set the example for our generation. He, like all of us, dealt with the difficulties of this life, but Joe was always solid. He, too, embraced the faith of our fathers and I will always think of him seated in the "triple branch reclining spot" of our family. He also was the best baseball player in the family. I have always admired and respected him, not only for the way he lived, but also for the way he died. I was fortunate to be with him in his hospital room just hours before he died. He asked me to speak at his memorial service and he made sure that all of us knew that he had complete assurance of his salvation. It was a precious moment that I will always cherish.

We Parris cousins were blessed to have been born when, where, and to whom we were born. Our roots are grounded in God's Word and our family wholeheartedly believed it, accepted it, and made it the basis for living life. I do not have one bad childhood memory and my "cousin-brothers" helped me to be a blessed only child, and I think I am well adjusted.

CHAPTER 7

The Desire to Excel

When the news of my decision to enter the ministry became public, I was contacted by Bill Burnett who, at that time, was the coordinator of Fellowship of Christian Athletes in the state of Arkansas. Yes, that's the same Bill Burnett who was an All-American running back for the Arkansas Razorbacks. He had read about my decision in a Baptist publication. He congratulated me on the decision and then said, "Stan, I just want you to consider that there is no profession that has more of an opportunity to have a positive influence on young people than a Christian coach." He was not trying to talk me out of the vocational ministry path, but rather was encouraging me to make sure about the clarity of the calling. I appreciated his concern and I could not agree more with his statement about coaches. I love coaches, especially Christian coaches.

There were several who had a significant impact on my life. In fact, I never had a bad coach and had a good relationship with all of them. *CHARLIE DONALDSON WAS ONE OF HIS COACHES —*

After high school, I was recruited by and had scholarship offers from several universities. A few came to my high school to talk with me, but only one came to my house. Coach Clyde Berry was the recently named head football coach at Henderson State in 1967. He came to our house "just outside of Hope," sat in our living room with my parents, told me that I would have a chance to start as a freshman, and prayed for me and my parents before he left. I visited a few other universities, but in my heart, I knew that I belonged at Henderson State. I don't remember thinking about pros and cons or stressing over the decision ... going to Henderson just felt right.

In hindsight, I think I wanted to be close to my parents and Henderson was only 50 miles away. At that time at National Collegiate Athletic Association (NCAA) Division I schools, freshmen were not allowed to play in varsity games, and I did not want to stand on the sidelines. I also knew that in my inconsistent and undisciplined spiritual condition, I needed to be around a Christian coach, and I believed that Coach Berry's prayer in our living room had been genuine.

I reported for "two-a-days" in August 1967 ... along with 130 others. The Vietnam War was in full swing and a lot of guys were looking for ways to secure student deferments to avoid the draft. An entirely new coaching staff meant a fresh opportunity to earn one of the 33 scholarships that could legally be given. Of course, some of those had already been given to upper class teammates, but there was always the chance of winning a position and earning a scholarship. I'm pretty sure the coaching staff did not expect 130 guys to show up for practices. There was not enough equipment for everyone to have the right size shoes, helmets, or shoulder pads. Helmets, especially, had to be shared, along with equipment lockers. Initially, we practiced three times a day. Offensive players would go first, leave the field, change clothes, and make room for defensive players. Even when we were divided up, some players still did not have helmets. This process was repeated all day long and practices were designed not only to find the best players, but also to "thin the herd." The dorms were packed with three-six players in a room. The attrition rate was high as many saw the odds of making the team and headed back home. You could hear cars starting up and leaving the parking lot at all hours of the night. One guy left his roommates a note that said, "Headed back to Texas. Give 'em hell!"

Even though Henderson State was a small National Association of Intercollegiate Athletics (NAIA) school, there were potential players there from many different parts of the country. Texas, Oklahoma, Louisiana, Alabama, West Virginia, New York, New Jersey, Florida, and many Arkansas towns were all represented. We even had a placekicker from Denmark. It goes without saying that there were some very interesting characters in the group. The Braddock twins from Florida came to Henderson as "walk-on's," hoping to make the team and earn a much-needed scholarship. Ronnie was a running back and Donnie was a linebacker. When Ronnie injured his ankle and was unable to practice, his brother filled in for him. The coaches could not tell them apart. During those two-a-day and three-a-day practices, Donnie was practicing with both groups, as a running back with the offense and as a linebacker with the defense. Thanks to Donnie's efforts they were both offered scholarships.

Coach Berry was our leader ... there was never any doubt about that. He was stern and his eyes were always invigorating, almost jumping with excitement. He always looked you directly in the eyes, which, at times, could be extremely intimidating. He had a coach's voice and could be heard on both ends of the field. He was a good motivator and must have had a good knowledge of the game because we had good teams. In fact, in 1969 we won the Arkansas Intercollegiate Conference Championship and most of the players on that team had showed up as "walk-on's" three years earlier. He was always reminding us that we must have "the desire to excel."

Early on a Saturday morning before a crucial conference game, we were all summoned to the cafeteria for a meeting. The minute we walked in we knew it was serious. Dr. Tilley, our team doctor, Coach Berry, and his eight-year-old son, Trey, had been returning from a recruiting trip on Friday night when their plane had crashed. Dr. Tilley, the pilot, had been killed instantly. Knowing they were about to crash, they stuffed Trey under the seats, and he was unharmed. Coach Berry survived with several broken ribs, a serious puncture wound in his eye, and a severely crushed hip. Coach Berry instructed Trey to run for help. The plane was still hanging in a tree. Eight-year-old Trey climbed out of the wreckage, made his way down the tree and ran toward a light in the distance. When help arrived, Coach Berry had lost consciousness and fallen to the ground, causing further injuries. Those injuries required at least five surgeries and lots of physical therapy, but Coach was back for the following season, with a noticeable limp, but with the same excitement in his eyes. That would be his last season as the head football coach, but a few years later after receiving his doctorate, he returned to Henderson State as a professor in the Physical Education Department. Later he would return to coaching, this time as the head baseball coach. The baseball field at Henderson is named in his honor.

As players, we watched Coach Berry deal with this life-changing incident with the same determination that he required of us on the playing field. But many of us had been watching him for the three years before the plane crash. We watched him with his three sons, Trey, Jay, and Clay. We watched how he lived his life in the community. We listened as he led us in prayer before practices. We especially watched his interaction with the middle son, Jay, who had muscular dystrophy and who would pass away at age 15. I know there were many times when he found himself "just outside of hope," but it was his faith and his relationship with the Father that strengthened him and enabled him to continue to influence young men.

For me, personally, there were times when he talked to me sternly, like a father, and at other times, when he would display incredible understanding. He knew my family history and he knew "the desire to excel" should apply not only to athletic efforts, but also to spiritual efforts. I always felt that he could read my conscience and that perhaps he knew of my inner spiritual struggles.

When I made the decision to enter the ministry in 1974, I wanted him to know that my inner struggle was over and when I told him, he was one of the few people who was not totally surprised.

Coach has followed our ministry through the years, especially our years spent in Venezuela as missionaries. At one point, he made a financial donation that allowed us to buy two horses for a Venezuelan Baptist Camp. There was also enough money to buy baseball equipment.

Bill Burnett's comment about the impact of Christian coaches is still true today and their impact can last for a lifetime. Coach Berry, who was 89 when last we talked, and was dealing with some new health issues, but his faith is still solid and his concern for the spiritual life of his players is stronger than ever. Thanks, Coach, for what you mean to me and countless others.

CHAPTER 8

The Other Love

There is a part of my Christian life of which I am not proud. I received eternal life through faith in Jesus at age nine. I have always had assurance of my salvation. I never really grew in my Christian life during the teen and college years. I was in church on a regular basis while at home with my parents, but I lacked the maturity, the strength, and even the desire to say no to temptations. It was a miserable existence. I would feel terrible about what I was doing, ask God to forgive me, pledge to change my lifestyle, and head right back into it at the next opportunity. To add to my feelings of disappointing God and disappointing my parents was the fact that I knew God was "calling me into the ministry." For anyone unfamiliar with that terminology, it simply means that God's plan for my life involved the procla-mation of the Gospel of Jesus Christ and the "call" was easily heard in my head and in my heart no matter how hard I tried to silence it. At times it was much louder, but it was always there. The more I tried to get away from it the more I could hear it. The strong inner voice in my conscience would never go away, not completely. I carried this secret all through high school and college. No one, I promise you, no one knew about this inner struggle but me and God.

Charlotte and I met in college and were at the same place in our spiritual pilgrimage. We were two very immature Christians floundering around outside of God's will and feeling very convicted about it. I remember a conversation we had one night on a date. It was the closest I ever came to sharing with someone about my inner struggle. The gist of the conversation was that we were both Christians, we were both members of a Baptist church, and we both knew that we were not where we should be in our relationship with the Lord. I knew that night that we were right for each other. I was in love. We were married at the beginning of our junior year in college.

I also had another love. I loved football. Since high school, my plan and my goal for my life was to play professional football. I really had no other plan. Even though the odds of that happening were off the chart, that was my plan. I played four years at Henderson, making All-Conference all four years. I was named to the All-America team at the end of my senior year. In 1971, I signed a free agent contract with the Buffalo Bills of the National Football League. I was on track with my plan for my life.

I was in the Bills' training camp for six weeks. You've probably seen movies or heard about being a rookie and trying to make the team. It did not take me long to realize that this was not small college competition. There were only two other players in camp who had even heard of my alma mater. Each morning the trainers would walk down the hallways of the dorm shouting, "Wake up call," but at some doors they would stop, knock on the door, and say the dreaded, "Coach wants to see you. Bring your playbook." My two roommates were cut early in the training camp and after the first month, I was the only one left on my end of the hall.

Things were going well; even some of the veterans were talking to me and giving me rides back to the dorm. We had a Saturday afternoon scrimmage with more spectators in attendance than the crowds I had played in front of during college. I had a good scrimmage and after the scrimmage my position coach told me that I had made the team. They were going to keep me. I couldn't wait to get to the pay phone and call Charlotte back in Arkansas. I will never forget what I said to her, "We are moving to Buffalo!"

Monday morning the trainer once again came walking down the hall, but this time he was yelling, "Team meeting in 30 minutes." There was a lot of uncertainty about this unscheduled team meeting; even the veterans seemed to be in the dark. The announcement was that the Bills' owner had fired the head coach and named the personnel director to temporarily fill the position. This meant the final decision about the team roster had not yet been finalized. I quickly glanced across the room and made eye contact with the other rookie who was competing for the same position. He seemed happy.

That same Monday afternoon as practice ended, I was walking off the field and stepped into a sprinkler head hole straining my right knee. I had played 4 years of college football, 44 games, without a serious injury and in one accidental wrong step, my dream and plan of being a professional football player was over. I missed the entire next week of practice and the "other guy" was selected for the position. My position coach was kind and said that they would like for me to play a year in the Canadian League and come back for the next year. But somewhere in my heart there was this conviction that this was not where I needed to be. I thanked the coach and said, "Just give me a ticket to Little Rock, Arkansas."

I did not call Charlotte with the news, I just showed up at the door of our apartment in Arkansas. I had failed and my only plan for my life had ended. I was completely devastated.

My only purpose for sharing this story is to point out that sometimes we find ourselves "just outside of hope" because we position ourselves there. Ignoring and neglecting God's will for our lives will always lead to disappointment and a sense of hopelessness. I am quite sure you noticed the repetitive uses of the words "I," "me," and "my" as you read the account of my other love. There was no mention of God. In fact, there was absolute disobedience to the direction and calling of God for my life. That "accidental wrong step" was into a hole I had dug by myself through willful disobedience to God. God had not caused the failure nor was He responsible for the feeling of devastation, but that failure and that devastation would lead us on a three-year journey that would change everything about us and about finding God's will.

CHAPTER 9

The Short Straw

After being cut from the Buffalo Bills, I returned to Arkansas and immediately began the search for a coaching job. Football practices were already underway and most coaching positions were filled. However, I received a phone call from a head coach in Center, Texas, who had read in the Dallas Morning News that I had been released from the Bills. There was a vacancy on his staff and he offered me the job. The next day Charlotte and I drove the 200 miles to meet the coach and to be interviewed by the superintendent. Since football practice had already started and classes would begin soon, we were offered the job, signed the contract, and found an apartment ... all in one day.

We returned to Arkansas, packed everything we owned in a U-Haul trailer and headed into adulthood. We were in Texas for only 10 months, but during that time we had started attending church and acknowledged that it was time to seriously address the very anemic spiritual part of our marriage. The phone call came in late April that there were multiple coaching changes being made in my hometown of Hope. I was offered the defensive coordinator position for the Hope Bobcats and as the school year ended, we once again packed up our possessions, this time in a U-Haul truck, and headed back to Arkansas. By this time, I had convinced myself that God had "let me off the hook" with the call to ministry idea. This was a good job, we had a child, we were going to church, and I was a good coach ... I knew football.

Charlotte and I began to grow spiritually as we participated in small group Bible studies with other young couples. For the first time in my life the Bible really came alive. Charlotte and I began to internalize the truths we were being taught. The two years we spent coaching in Hope and participating in the ministries of First Baptist Church re-directed the path of our lives. Looking back on those two years, there were two obvious spiritual markers that changed everything. One was an unexpected event and the other was a new understanding of a spiritual principle.

The event occurred when a few of our football players approached the coaching staff about starting a Fellowship of Christian Athletes chapter at our school. The dilemma was that one of the coaches had to agree to be the sponsor of the group. I am not proud of this, but in a closed-door meeting, six grown men drew straws to see which one of us "had to be" the sponsor. I drew the short straw. I will be forever grateful to God for "losing" that draw.

The FCA group met weekly and as I listened to the testimonies and prayer concerns of these young men, there was strong conviction in my heart that there was still something missing in my life. Their commitment to Christ and their concern for their peers challenged my own spiritual life. There was one young man in particular whom I really admired. He was not a great athlete, but, at age 16, he had made the decision to be a preacher.

The spiritual principle introduced to us was presented in a tract entitled, *Have You Made The Wonderful Discovery Of The Spirit Filled Life?* by Bill Bright, president of Campus Crusade International. This teaching was life-changing for both Charlotte and me. As already mentioned, I became a Christian at age nine and had been an active church member through high school. I had heard hundreds of sermons, but had never understood the role of the Holy Spirit in my life. I knew that He was the third Person of the Trinity and that He was referred to as the Comforter. I knew nothing about the practicality of His presence in my life or of releasing control of my life to Him. Being filled with the Holy Spirit, being controlled by Him, was the most liberating truth I had ever heard. For years I had planned my life. For years I had tried with my most sincere efforts to be obedient, to resist temptation, to live the Christian life, but I had failed time and time again.

Learning the truth about being filled and living life in the Spirit took the focus off my doing and placed it on what Christ had already done. The unexpected event and the understanding of that principle led me to make the decision I had been afraid of and running from for many years. In April of 1974, I made the decision to resign from coaching and become a "full-time minister." Charlotte and I had no idea what that really meant and where it would lead us.

Note: The coach who hired me and gave me my first job was Phil Jones, who grew up in Hope, Arkansas. His twin brother, Ken, had been one of my coaches in college.

The night before I made the decision to "be a preacher," I spent a couple of hours talking and praying with a dear friend who owned a farm "just outside of Hope."

CHAPTER 10

The Arrows Are Beyond You

A "call to missions" was never, ever on my radar … I mean never, ever. I did not grow up hearing about missionaries or being exposed to missionary stories. While in seminary, I attended a chapel service led by Foreign Missionaries (a term later changed to International Missionaries) that included a challenge and an invitation to accept the call to become a missionary. The student sitting next to me sprang from his seat and literally ran to the altar, crying uncontrollably as he "surrendered to the call." Honestly, at the time, that entire experience frightened me and I left that chapel service convinced that missions was something for others, but not for me.

After seminary, our first pastorate was in Coolidge, Arizona. While there, our church participated in a Missions Conference that involved many churches in our area and missionary speakers from different parts of the United States and the world. The speakers were very interesting, but, for me, the impact of the conference was the personal time spent with them. I found them to be extremely human, theologically sound, passionate about evangelism, and having a world vision that surpassed that of most Christians, myself included. At the end of the week, one of the missionaries said to me, "I'll see you in Costa Rica in two years." It was a statement made just before the missionary got into the car to leave and I don't think either of us realized the impact that statement would have.

Several weeks passed and that missionary's parting words were still in my mind. I mentioned this to Charlotte, but she was not at all positive about leaving the pastorate and becoming missionaries. At that point in our journey there were legitimate reasons for her hesitancy. She grew up listening to missionary speakers, reading the biographies of missionaries, and participating in missionary education activities in her church. She had actually made a decision as an 11-year-old to "surrender my life to fulfill the Great Commission." Serving in a local church as a pastor's wife was an obvious way to honor the commitment she had made as a child. Charlotte was way ahead of me in understanding the practical aspects of becoming missionaries. She knew how much I loved preaching and there was the obstacle of language learning and trying to accurately communicate the Gospel in another language. We had three children ages ten, seven, and one. She was thinking of my parents and the fact that I was an only child and more importantly, our children were my parents' only grandchildren. Honestly, her hesitation was not about her commitment or readiness, it was about our understanding of issues that I had never considered. She was right to allow more time for God to further prepare us.

We remained in Arizona for two-and-a-half years before moving to Oklahoma City. Just as our Arizona church was the perfect first pastorate, our time in Oklahoma was perfect for the next step in our pilgrimage. In February 1982, Charlotte and I, along with 20 church members, participated in a Volunteer Missions Trip to Maracaibo, Venezuela. We were divided into different teams and assigned to work with several different local Baptist churches. We visited door-to-door in neighborhoods, sharing our testimonies through translators. We each had translated copies of our testimonies explaining how we came to trust in Christ, and explaining how it was a personal, individual decision. Each evening we had worship services where we preached through translators. During our time there, we saw over 2,000 Venezuelans trust in Jesus as their personal Savior.

No one in our group had ever experienced such a manifestation of God's presence and power. We witnessed entire families giving their lives to Jesus Christ. As we sat in one house, the translator was explaining that a curse had been placed on the women living there. Since the curse, there had been years of sexual abuse from neighborhood men. Three generations of women had suffered the abuse, believing that it was irreversible because of the curse. As the Gospel was explained, it became evident that one of the women was very interested and wanted to hear more, but there was an obvious struggle going on. Her countenance began to change; she appeared angry; others in the room became uncomfortable as we continued to read Scripture and explain the plan of salvation. Finally, the translator approached the woman and asked her if she wanted to receive Christ into her life. She nodded and our translator led her to pray, asking Jesus to break the curse and to bring salvation to her house. After she had prayed, she lifted her face, her countenance was completely changed, she was smiling, and her first words were, "It's gone."

As we continued our visits, we met a young 18-year-old, who was working as a maid in one of the homes. I could tell that she was having a very difficult time understanding what we were trying to explain. She appeared confused and completely lost in the conversation. I asked one of my Venezuelan translators to clarify what was happening. Her words would change my life and the direction of my ministry. She said, "This young lady is a Guajira (an indigenous group living in Venezuela and Colombia) and she has never heard of God." Never heard of God? Standing in front of that house on a Venezuelan street corner, God spoke to my heart about His heart. I caught a glimpse, just a glimpse, of the true meaning of John 3:16, verse I had known since childhood. *"For God so loved the world, that He gave His only begotten Son, that whosoever believes in Him, will not perish, but have everlasting life."* (NASB) I could not get the picture of that young Guajira girl out of my mind.

On the plane trip home, Charlotte and I agreed that it was time to seek God's will about a call to become missionaries. It did not take long for confirmation of our call to become evident.

As a couple, we have always sought confirmation of God's will by using three methods. The counsel of Spirit-filled believers, the opening and closing of doors of opportunity, and the receiving of a "word from God" ... a verse or passage of Scripture that speaks directly to our hearts. All three methods are usually in agreement, but the final confirmation for us has always been from God's Word. Upon returning from our Venezuelan Mission Trip, I contacted the International Mission Board just to express our interest and ask questions about the next steps. I was told that one of the top five requests for missionaries was in Maracaibo, Venezuela. Wow! We began to discuss with a few close friends the direction we felt God was leading us and none of them were surprised. They had sensed that God might be leading us to become missionaries. Wow!

The real confirmation came on a Sunday night as I was preaching from 1 Samuel 20. The passage deals with David's difficult decision concerning his future. Was he to remain with his friend, Jonathan, or was it God's will for him to exchange the security of the familiar for the uncertainty of the unknown? As you read the chapter, the plan unfolds: *Then Jonathan said to him, "Tomorrow is the new moon, and you will be missed because your seat will be empty. When you have stayed for three days, you shall go down quickly and come to the place where you hid yourself on that eventful day, and you shall remain by the stone Ezel. I will shoot three arrows to the side, as though I shot at a target. And behold, I will send the lad, saying, 'Go, find the arrows.' If I specifically say to* the lad, 'Behold, the arrows are on this side of you, get them, ' then come; for there is safety for you and no harm, as the LORD lives. But if I say to the youth, 'Behold, the arrows are beyond you,' go, for the LORD has sent you away." (1 Samuel 20:18-22 NASB)

The story continues in verse 35: "Now it came about in the morning that Jonathan went out into the field for the appointment with David, and a little lad was with him. He said to his lad, "Run, find now the arrows which I am about to shoot." As the lad was running, he shot an arrow past him. When the lad reached the place of the arrow which Jonathan had shot, Jonathan called after the lad and said, "Is not the arrow beyond you?" And Jonathan called after the lad, "Hurry, be quick, do not stay!" And Jonathan's lad picked up the arrow and came to his master. But the lad was not aware of anything; only Jonathan and David knew about the matter. Then Jonathan gave his weapons to his lad and said to him, "Go, bring them to the city." When the lad was gone, David rose from the south side and fell on his face to the ground, and bowed three times. And they kissed each other and wept together, but David wept the more. Jonathan said to David, "Go in safety, inasmuch as we have sworn to each other in the name of the LORD, saying, 'The LORD will be between me and you, and between my descendants and your descendants forever.'" Then he rose and departed, while Jonathan went into the city." (1 Samuel 20:35-42 NASB) "Is not the arrow beyond you?" was our call to missions.

As I was reading this passage in that Sunday night worship service, Charlotte and I made eye contact and we knew in that moment that we had received the confirmation. It was time for us to leave the convenience of the familiar and trust God in the uncertainty of the future. We made official contact with the International Mission Board in February and we were appointed as missionaries to Venezuela in July 1982.

This journey actually began with an 11-year-old Charlotte "surrendering her life to fulfill the Great Commission." Definitely a seed had been planted with the missionary's comment, "I'll see you in Costa Rica in two years." The real spiritual marker was the Volunteer Mission Trip and, for me, meeting an 18-year-old girl who had never heard of God. That encounter changed me. After 45 years of ministry that includes seven years in Venezuela, and over 50 mission trips to dozens of countries, I have never forgotten her face or the conviction that she and others like her are "just outside of hope."

CHAPTER 11

Our Best vs. God's Best

After my wife and I felt God's call to missions, one of our first stops was in San Jose, Costa Rica, where we attended a year of language school. We arrived in Costa Rica soon after Christmas 1982 with our three children, seven suitcases, five carry-ons, and seven footlockers. We would spend the next 11 months studying the Spanish language and culture and adapting to a new lifestyle.

One of the hardest adjustments for us was coming to grips with the fact that we were, for the very first time in either of our lives, considered wealthy. Even though we were living in a 900 square-foot bungalow, had no transportation, and were making fewer dollars than we had made in several years, we were still better off than most of our Costa Rican neighbors.

Because we were "wealthy" and because the language school schedule was very intense, it was suggested that each missionary family have a maid. Carmen was an "empleada" who had years of experience working for missionaries as they spent their year in language school before going on to their assigned countries. She was a great cook and housekeeper and it was nice to come home from language school to one of her home-cooked meals. The laundry would be just about dry and Carmen would bring it in from the clothesline just minutes before the rain started. During the rainy season, precipitation would begin around one o'clock and sometimes last until late at night. With classes all morning and assignments that required us to go out in the afternoons to experience the culture, Carmen was a necessity and a great blessing to our family. We were just not accustomed to having a maid.

As the months passed and our Spanish improved, we learned more and more about Carmen and her two daughters. She was a Christian and faithfully attended her evangelical church. She really was a delight to our family, and we grew to love her and wanted to help her in any way we could. Her oldest daughter, Claudia, was 12 years old and was legally blind. Because of her limited vision, she had struggled in school and had been unable to keep up with her classmates. We prayed about this situation and after sending her to an optometrist for evaluation, decided a good thing to do would be to buy Claudia a pair of glasses and pay for a tutor to help her catch up with her studies. Carmen was elated at the idea and soon Claudia was seeing and reading and her classes with the tutor were going well. I don't think we were ever prideful about what we had been able to do with some of our extra money, but we felt that this was the right thing to do and we were happy that God had given us an opportunity to help such special people. It was the least we could do and the best idea we came up with for helping Carmen and her family.

One Monday morning when Carmen arrived at our house, Claudia came running into the house ahead of her mother. She was obviously excited about something and as she screamed in her excitement we were struggling to understand what she was saying in Spanish. I couldn't understand her, but I did notice that she was not wearing her glasses and immediately I assumed that she had either lost or broken those glasses. I remember doing the math in my head to see if we would be able to afford another pair for her before our next paycheck. Finally, when Carmen made it into the house, she was able to explain it all to us in a much calmer and slower Spanish.

While attending church on Sunday, Claudia had responded to her pastor's invitation for people to come to the front of the church and kneel if they had special prayer requests. Claudia went to her pastor and requested that he pray for her eyesight. He did and in that moment her eyes were healed, and her vision was completely restored. What she was so excited about and what she was trying to tell us was that she no longer needed those glasses. She could see.

I have never forgotten what God spoke to my heart in that moment. He said, "You did the best you could do. You did all you could do. But I want you to understand as you begin this missionary career that it is never about what you can do. You need to trust me and never be content with doing your best. My people deserve the best that I can do." I have never forgotten the excitement on Claudia's face as she experienced what only God could have done. It has been my desire since that day to see that same glowing, joyful face in the lives of people as they encounter the supernatural power of God.

Note: Pray that you will never settle for the best you can do, but that people in your world will know the joy of experiencing what only God can do in their circumstances. Zechariah 4:6 — Then he answered and said to me, *"This is the word of the LORD to Zerubbabel saying, 'Not by might nor by power, but by My Spirit,' says the LORD of hosts."* (NASB)

CHAPTER 12

A Painful Decision

During our Language School assignment in San José, Costa Rica, my parents decided to visit us. This was a huge decision considering neither of them had ever been outside the United States, and the fact that my mother had never flown on an airplane. The motivation of seeing your three grandchildren can cause you to overcome great fear and do things that may have seemed very unlikely. At the time Dad was 71 and Mother was 68 (that seemed a lot older to me then than it does now). It was quite the accomplishment since in 1983, not only were there no direct flights, there was no easy itinerary. Their flights took them from New Orleans-Belize-El Salvador-Nicaragua-Costa Rica. It was quite the experience.

They had planned their trip to correspond with the Language School's trimester break, so we were free to visit and show them some of the beautiful sites of San José. Mother really surprised us with her excitement and interest in visiting some of the well-known national buildings and museums. They also enjoyed meeting some of our neighbors, attending our church, and meeting some of our missionary colleagues.

While they were with us, Mother mentioned a few times that she had been experiencing a sharp pain. She promised that she would make a doctor's appointment as soon as they returned home. A few weeks later, we received the phone call that her cancer had returned and that she would begin treatments immediately.

We had not yet finished the last trimester of our language study, but we were allowed to return to the U.S. to spend time with my parents. Mother was deteriorating rapidly from the very aggressive cancer. We had already been granted entry visas into Venezuela, but we had to enter the country by January 12 or the visas would be invalidated. We were able to spend the month of December with her, but those days were filled with hospital stays, her extreme reaction to the chemotherapy, and increasing weakness. By Christmas we all knew that unless God chose to heal her, the time of her departure would be soon.

As the deadline date of January 12 grew closer, we were faced with a painful decision. We were confident of our call to Venezuela, but would we be able to board the plane knowing the impact it would have on our entire family.

Mother was placed back into the hospital right after Christmas. During one of our visits, I was seated at her bedside when she told me that she was ready to go to heaven. She also told me that she knew that God had called us, and that God's will was for us to be in Venezuela. She said, "I want you to go."

I will never forget my last conversation with her on January 11, 1984. I prayed, we hugged, and she said, "Go, and don't worry about me." I did not cry until I made it to the stairwell and then the tears flowed uncontrollably. I was alone in that stairwell of the hospital, but all the cherished memories of my mother flooded my heart with peace and thankfulness.

We boarded the plane the next morning after what had been a very emotional six weeks. At times we had felt as if we were "just outside of hope," but the prayers of the people of God, the promises of the Word of God, and the confidence of my mother in the assurance of her salvation, renewed our hope and enabled us to "Go."

Mother departed this life on January 26, 1984, just two weeks after that painful goodbye.

I have often thought about those emotional and stressful weeks. I am thankful that Mother was willing to make that decision to ensure that we would not have to make it. We have Biblical hope that we will see her again and I will get to thank her personally for her sacrifice.

*The weather vane on top of the steeple at First Baptist Church in Hope,
Arkansas. "No matter which way the wind is blowing, God is still God
and there is always hope."*

A poverty stricken community in Pakistan. One of these precious girls had the sweetest smile and the dirtiest feet I had ever seen.

My first meeting with "Amet" in a Turkish orphanage. There was an immediate connection.

(Above) The sewing ministry in Turkey provided a ray of hope for many women whose lives had been dramatically changed by the 1999 earthquake.

(Below) It was a steep 45-minute hike up the trail to this remote Chinese village. When I finally arrived, this lady smiled and said to me, "Welcome to our home, older person."

(Above) Just outside of hope, and possibly not much time for us to reach the nations with the Gospel.

(Below) In the shade of this mango tree, a church was planted that brought new hope to an entire community.

(Above) A picture is worth a thousand ... prayers.

(Below) These children had never heard of Jesus, but they have now heard about Him and His love for their village.

CHAPTER 13

The Effectual Fervent Prayer

Charlotte and I moved our family to Maracaibo, Venezuela, in 1984 to work with Venezuelan Baptist churches. We lived on a dead-end street in a very nice part of the city. Our children quickly made friends with our neighbors' children and spent a lot of time in their homes. Our daughter, who was 10 at the time, came home one day saying that the maid next door had been singing some of the same songs we knew and sang in the Baptist churches. Charlotte had an over-the-fence meeting with Arlenis to hear her story. She was a creyente (believer) and lived in a neighborhood some distance away. She was thrilled to know that we were in Venezuela to start new churches. Arlenis told Charlotte that for two years she had been praying for a church to be started in her neighborhood. She gave us directions and invited us, implored us, to visit her and her family. We had no idea what awaited us there.

With great effort and divine intervention, we were able to find where she lived. There were no roads, no electricity, no water, no sewers, and certainly no churches. Arlenis and her family lived in the poorest, most neglected, and most unsafe area of the city. We found her house and had just started the conversation when she pointed to the land across the "street" and told us with great enthusiasm that it was for sale. A few months later we purchased that property and began meeting under a mango tree. It was the beginning of what is today the New Hope

Baptist Church. The church is there today because of the persistent praying of one humble lady. Most people would probably say that this neighborhood was "way outside of hope," but one person knew that a new hope was available through the proclamation of the Gospel.

Poverty has a very distinct odor. I have smelled it in many different countries, and it smells the same. It smells like despair with a hint of no-way-out of hopelessness.

2 Corinthians 2:14-15: "*But thanks be to God, who always leads us in triumph, and manifests through us the sweet aroma of the knowledge of Him in every place. For we are a fragrance for Christ to God among those who are being saved and among those who are perishing,*" (NASB)

Our friend, Arlenis, knew that the neighborhood needed water, electricity, and sanitation, but she knew that the real difference maker would be the hope that only the Gospel could bring. God is the author of hope. The only people who are without hope are those who are without God. The fragrance of Christ was much needed in the neighborhood.

We began to meet people who were not that far away from hope; they just didn't know it. Because of God's love and mercy and because of Arlenis' prayers, we began to meet people in whom God was already at work. Hope was moving closer to this neighborhood.

On most weekdays, I would go to the neighborhood and just walk the "streets," greeting the people and praying. This was before the term "Prayer-Walking" was introduced, but it certainly describes what I was doing.

A lot of my praying was for my own safety. Charlotte and I have discussed with hindsight whether we would have ever gone into that area had we been aware of the dangers. A lot of the people living there were in Venezuela illegally and drug movements from neighboring Colombia were common. The neighborhood had "sprung up "about 10 years earlier by large numbers of people "invading" the unoccupied land. By the time authorities had been notified, there were too many people who had already built simple dwellings ("ranchitos") and moved into them. Plus, there was really no other place for them in the already overcrowded city of two-million people. We estimated at least 2,000 people living in this neighborhood, which consisted of about 10 square blocks.

I'm not saying that I was the first white person they had ever seen, but I am fairly certain that I was the first one to walk the "streets" of their neighborhood. I was even more of an oddity because of my 6-foot-5-inch frame. Let's just say I stood out!

Curiosity among the neighborhood residents was even more increased when we showed up on Sunday mornings with our three children to have church under the mango tree. Needless to say, news spread quickly and there was much interest and much suspicion.

Soon after I began "prayer walking" the neighborhood, I was approached by a man well-known in the area as, "El Cali," a reference to his native city of Cali, Colombia. He was known as a "malandro," which probably translates as "a bad dude." He was short in stature, but he had a very serious and stern look about him. People in the area feared him. He walked up to me and said in Spanish, "How much did that watch cost?" I told him exactly what I had paid for it. I had been advised against wearing anything of value and always to carry very little cash, but to always carry some and to give it up willingly if robbed. He expressed no interest in my $20 watch.

His next question was, "Who are you and what are you doing in my neighborhood?" We had been in Venezuela for only a few months and my language skills were still limited, but I was able to communicate that I was there to share God's message of hope through faith in Jesus Christ. His next statement surprised me, "You don't have to worry about a thing, I will make sure you are safe here."

After that first encounter, I would occasionally see him in the neighborhood, and he was always friendly. I was surprised one Sunday when he attended our afternoon worship service and even more surprised when he responded to the invitation we always gave at the end of the service.

He told me that he wanted to give his life to Christ. He said his mother was a believer in Colombia and he knew that she had never stopped praying for him. He confessed that for years he had been a "mule," backpacking drugs across the border into Venezuela. The previous week, policemen had pursued him, shooting at him. At one point, they had him cornered with his hands in the air and they intended to kill him. He watched bullet after bullet fall short and drop into the sand by his side. The policemen let him go. He told me that he believed God had spared his life because of his mother's prayers. That day he trusted in Jesus as his Savior. His is one of many stories of changed lives we would eventually see in that neighborhood.

During the next several years, we would meet and be impacted by some of the sweetest, most humble people on the face of the earth. They accepted our presence in their neighborhood and even became very protective of us and of the message we were sharing.

It all began with the effective fervent prayers of our neighbor's maid.

CHAPTER 14

First Fruits

The first person in the neighborhood to publicly receive Christ as personal Savior was a young mother named Sophia. When I first began to "prayer walk" in the neighborhood, there was a mixture of curiosity and suspicion. As I mentioned, this was not a neighborhood accustomed to seeing North Americans walk their streets. Some would respond to "Buenos Días" or other greetings, others would just nod or look away. Because it was a dangerous area, initially my walking in any direction was within three or four blocks of the home of Arlemis, our friend. After walking, I would come back to her house, sit under her shade tree, and drink her delicious Colombian coffee. I would ask her about different houses or people I had seen or met.

At one house, a young lady, Sophia, was always outside washing clothes when I walked past. Since there was no water service in the neighborhood, water trucks would come daily and sell water, pumping it into large barrels. That water was used for drinking, cooking, bathing, and washing clothes.

Sophia would watch intently as I walked by her house each day. Her house was a typical "ranchito," one room, boards nailed together, tin roof, dirt floor. There was another simple structure outside where she cooked over a charcoal fire. Sophia was from Colombia, but she also was part Guajira. The Guajira are an indigenous people group, who have dual citizenship in Colombia and Venezuela. They have lived for centuries in the frontier between the two countries and many of them survive by selling contraband brought into the country. They have their own language, their own culture, and for the most part they are not a religious people.

One morning Sophia saw me coming down her street and she walked slowly toward the barbed wire fence that marked the front of their property. For the first time, I stopped in front of her house and introduced myself. "May I ask you a question?" she said. "Over one year ago I woke up very early in the morning and could not sleep. It was so hot, and I walked outside to see if it might be cooler. As I was standing there, I looked up at the sky and I saw something written in the stars. I ran back into the house and woke up my husband. I made him come outside and I pointed to the writing in the sky, but he could not see it. He never saw it, but it was very clear to me. I have been waiting for someone to come and explain to me the words that I saw written in the sky and I think you are that person." I asked her to please tell me what she had seen. She said, "I saw two words. It said 'Jesus Saves.' Can you tell me what that means?"

For the next 30 minutes we stood at the fence and in my very "rookie" Spanish, I shared with her the Good News of the Gospel of Jesus Christ. She did not question one statement or one verse of Scripture, she just kept smiling and nodding her head. She did not hesitate to ask Jesus to forgive her of her sin and take complete control of her life. I will never forget the smile that came over her face on that morning in 1984.

It took me a while to process what had transpired that day. This experience was way outside my theological comfort zone. I believed that God could use any methods He desired to reach those who were "just outside of hope," but at this point in our ministry, I had very little experience with this kind of supernatural manifestation of God's power.

Sophia was the first "spiritual fruit" in this neighborhood, but she would not be the last. Neither would this be the last of God's supernatural manifestations. God will go to great lengths to share that Jesus Saves with those who are "just outside of hope."

Note: A few months later, Sophia would share her testimony with others in the neighborhood and she would always say that "Brother Stan explained this to me in perfect Spanish." Yet another supernatural manifestation of God's power.

CHAPTER 15

Won Without a Word

As the attendance grew at the Sunday morning Bible Study, the shade under the mango tree was no longer large enough. The climate in Maracaibo is hot, always hot. There are no seasons so there is never any real relief from the heat, but at least a roof over your head provides some relief from what some Venezuelans refer to as "the angry sun." It was time to think about some kind of structure that we could call a church building.

A pastor in the city told us about a vacant portable building that his church was no longer using and assured us that we could have it, if we could move it. I only wish that we had videoed our crew disassembling, loading, moving, and reassembling the building. One of my greatest memories is of a pastor, our 14-year-old son, and myself holding up the roof as the side panels were being disassembled. We were balancing the roof with three long poles, much like the old routine of the juggler attempting to balance the plates on thin sticks. During one treacherous moment, our pastor-friend voiced the statement that would become the "go-to phrase" for our family. As we held up the roof, the sides were removed and we were supporting the entire weight and shuffling our feet to keep it from crashing, Pastor Juan calmly muttered the famous words, "Si se cae, se cae" … if it falls, it falls. Those words became the Parris motto.

The building was perfect for the neighborhood and we began having Sunday morning and Sunday afternoon worship services.

We could raise the side panels, leave the front and back doors open and, on rare occasions, actually get a little breeze. However, the greatest advantage to the open doors and windows was that the neighbors could hear the singing and the preaching of God's Word.

Living in the house just behind the back door was a family of five — Henry, Marta, and their three little girls. I would see Marta almost every day as I prayer-walked the neighborhood. The opportunity finally came to present the Gospel to her, and she had a lot of questions. We had several meetings before she willingly prayed to trust in Jesus alone for eternal life.

Marta was extremely excited about her newfound faith, but Henry let it be known that he was not in agreement with her decision. He had not married an "evangélica" (a non-Catholic believer) and had no intention of allowing those teachings in his home. He would not allow Marta to attend our church and he certainly would not allow her to indoctrinate their daughters.

Marta asked me what she should do. I asked her to read a passage of Scripture, to pray about the meaning of the passage, and then, when we met the next time, I would try to answer any questions she might have. The passage was 1 Peter 3:1-6: *"In the same way, you wives, be submissive to your own husbands so that even if any of them are disobedient to the word, they may be won without a word by the behavior of their wives, as they observe your chaste and respectful behavior. Your adornment must not be merely external braiding the hair, and wearing gold jewelry, or putting on dresses; but let it be the hidden person of the heart, with the imperishable quality of a gentle and quiet spirit, which is precious in the sight of God. For in this way in former times the holy women also, who hoped in God, used to adorn themselves, being submissive to their own husbands; just as Sarah obeyed Abraham, calling him lord, and you have become her children if you do what is right without being frightened by any fear."* (NASB)

It did not take Marta long to understand what she was being asked to do. She would not go against the wishes of her husband. She would not attend our worship services, she would not read the Bible out loud in the presence of her children, but she would read it silently to herself. She also decided to do the family's laundry on Sunday mornings while standing in their back yard just outside the back door of our building. She was there every Sunday morning.

In just a short period of time, Henry noticed changes in his wife. He told her it would be okay for her to read the Bible out loud for the children. He began to sit in on the readings and then he gave her and their daughters permission to come to church. For several years that was their agreement, and finally the day came when Henry gave his life to Christ. Years later, after we had returned to the United States, we learned that Henry and Marta were in charge of the Children's Ministry in the church.

Several obvious things stand out about Marta's story. She was radically changed when she received Jesus as her Savior. Those changes were used by God to bring her husband to Truth. Even though she found herself in a delicate situation with her non-believing husband, she wholeheartedly believed in and trusted in God's Word. She is a great example of a person who is "just outside of hope," but closer than she thought she was. She was literally standing at the back door of hope for herself and for her family. It was her faith in a promise she read in God's Word that allowed her husband to "be won without a word." I have always had the greatest respect for her obedience to the Word of God.

CHAPTER 16

A Remarkable Testimony

first met Blanca Rosa Cassanova Jimenez in Maracay, Venezuela, in 1987. I was translating for a missions team from the United States that was in-country for a one-week evangelism emphasis. We were visiting door-to-door in one of the neighborhoods when we knocked on the door of this remarkable woman, who shared her remarkable story of how God had worked in her life. I have kept my hand-written notes from that visit with Blanca for over 30 years, and I tried to record her story exactly the way she shared it with us during our visit to her home.

Her story begins in 1962 when Blanca was sentenced to 20 years in prison in her homeland of Cuba. She, her husband, and father had been falsely accused by the Cuban government of collaborating with the CIA. Her husband and her father were both shot to death in prison by the authorities, along with 300 other men, because of their presumed political activities. While in prison she was repeatedly beaten and tortured. She spent a year and a half in a military hospital in Havana as a result of the beatings she suffered at the hands of the prison officials. She described to us in detail how her left arm had been broken and how her forehead had been split open due to beatings with a pistol.

Because of the severity of her injuries and because the authorities did not want her to die while in their custody, she was granted "provisional liberty" and released from prison after serving 12 years of her sentence. She was taken to another hospital where the doctors decided to operate even though her condition was so serious that she was not expected to survive the surgery.

It was the night before the operation that Blanca had a dream. In the dream she was lying in her bed looking upward. She was looking up at a door with a window above it. Jesus was looking down at her through that window. She could see His face. And, in His face, she could sense His concern and His love for her. In her dream, Jesus came to that window three times, and each time He would peer down at her and shake His head from side to side as if He was saying, "No." Blanca determined in her mind that Jesus was telling her that she was not going to die. She went to sleep and slept peacefully.

The next morning when the doctor who was going to perform the operation came to examine her, he found that she had been completely healed of her injuries. Not knowing how to explain what had occurred and after concurring with other doctors, Blanca was released from the hospital and sent home. As she was preparing to leave the hospital her doctor made an unusual request. Knowing that her husband had been executed and knowing that Blanca had no children, he asked her if she would be interested in adopting a three-day old baby boy whose mother did not want him and whose father was in prison. She took her new son and went home.

At this point in her life Blanca was not a Christian. In fact, she had never heard the Gospel until a few months after being healed by God and released from the hospital. Invited by a friend to attend an evangelical church, she met other Christians who explained to her how to receive Jesus as her Savior. Blanca explained to us that day how some Peruvian missionaries had discipled her and suggested to her pastor that she should be baptized. Her baptism was a very emotional and moving experience for her. She continued to faithfully attend the small evangelical church until she received a visit from government authorities, who reminded her that she still, technically, had a prison sentence to serve. The authorities warned her that if she continued to participate in the church activities, she would be placed back into prison.

For the next several years, some of the Christian women from that church would secretly visit her at night and they would gather together in her bedroom to worship.

When her adopted son, Jose Oriol, was six years old, she once again received a visit from the authorities. The boy's father, who was still in prison, had asked to see him before his execution date. He wanted to give his son a necklace and ring that were some of his only possessions. What occurred at the prison that day was horrific. After giving the gifts to his son, whom he was seeing for the first time, he was shot to death. This six-year-old boy witnessed the execution of the man who was his father and immediately fell unconscious to the ground. He remained unconscious for the next eight days. He was later diagnosed with cerebral lesions and because of the traumatic effect upon him, Jose Oriol had severe learning disabilities.

In 1986, with hopes of leaving Cuba, Blanca wrote a letter to the President of Venezuela, Jaime Lusinchi, asking for a visa to enter Venezuela. Within two months she received a personal reply from President Lusinchi granting her a visa and permission to come to Venezuela. As she and Jose Oriol were ready to board the plane, government officials advised her to leave all her possessions behind. She boarded the plane with her then-12-year-old son and arrived in her new country with no money and no possessions.

After arriving in her new country, she went from house to house asking for food to feed her son. She was told about a group of Cubans living in a small community in central Venezuela. After moving to that community, she initially found work as a caretaker for an apartment complex. As we visited with her on that summer day in 1987, drinking coffee and listening to her emotional story, we felt the presence of God in that small simple home. I felt at the time that we were sent to her door because she needed to share her story with those with whom she felt a kindred spirit. At that time there were no churches in her part of town.

Something else amazing happened that afternoon that left all of us in tears of joy and praise. As we listened to her story, Jose Oriol became more and more comfortable with our presence. Before long he was sitting close by and eventually sitting on the floor next to my chair. As we concluded our visit and just as we were preparing to say goodbye, Blanca asked us if we would pray for Jose Oriol. We placed our hands on this young boy, prayed for him, and then he asked his mother if he could receive Jesus as His Savior. Needless to say it was a great day in heaven as one more chapter was added to this remarkable story.

CHAPTER 17

Stephanie's Story

I once heard a man describing some of the amazing characteristics of eagles. He described how eagles build their nests, care for their young, teach their young to fly, search for food, and how they die.

Eagles have a premonition when it's time for them to die. When that time comes, they will leave the nest and fly to a rock ... always a rock. They will fasten their talons on the front of the rock and look straight into the face of the setting or the rising sun ... and they will die. Feet securely fastened on a rock, looking into the face of the sun. Apparently, there is no fear or struggle. When it's time, they know what to do.

In June of 1989, we returned to my hometown of Hope, Arkansas, and to our home church, First Baptist. I soon met the Arnold family and their amazing daughter, Stephanie. She was 10 years old and had been diagnosed with Ewing's Sarcoma, a rare form of bone cancer. Her mom wrote, "What could have been the end of our happiness was the beginning of our Spiritual growth as a family."

They began a seven-year roller coaster experience that would include eight major surgeries in addition to six years of chemotherapy and radiation treatments. The testimony of this family as they walked through this devastating experience was "that God's Word became alive in ways we never dreamed possible."

Her Mom wrote: "Stephanie was well in 1991 just to be sick again in 1992. Well in 1993, sick again in 1994. Stephanie seemed to be well until Christmas of 1995 when the cancer spread everywhere. Jesus said to 'Fix our eyes not on what is seen, but what is unseen. For what is seen is temporary, but what is unseen is Eternal' (2 Corinthians 4:1). And that was what we did; we simply put our trust in God and not on what we saw. By January of 1996 Stephanie was really sick and, in a lot of pain, but God is God and He gave us this verse to hold on to: Psalm 27:13 'I would have despaired unless I had not believed that I would see the goodness of the Lord in the land of the living. Wait for the Lord. Be strong and let your heart take courage.'

"Four months later Stephanie was in the hospital and getting worse each day. God gave us this verse in Isaiah 54:10, 'For the mountains may be removed and hills may shake, but My loving-kindness will not be removed from you, and My covenant of peace will not be shaken says the Lord who has compassion on you.'

"On May 1, 1996, Stephanie became very sick. In the early morning hours of May 2nd, something strange began to happen. After seven years of pain, she had no pain. She had not sat up by herself in several months, but now she could. A true miracle was taking place right before our eyes. I asked her if she was afraid and she said, 'No, Mama, I've given it all to God and He will take care of me.' And then she said, 'I love you.' Those were her last words. Minutes later she sat up in the bed, reached past her Dad, for the eastern wall of her hospital and went into the arms of her Savior Jesus Christ. Just as the sun came up on May 2, 1996, Stephanie was completely healed in God's perfect way."

Feet on a rock. Looking straight into the face of the rising sun … or in Stephanie's case, into the face of the Son. No fear. No struggle.

I was honored to speak at her memorial service. I read the passage from Acts 7:55-56 about the death of Stephen — "But being full of the Holy Spirit, he gazed intently into heaven and saw the glory of God, and Jesus standing at the right hand of God; and he said, "Behold, I see the heavens opened up and the Son of Man standing at the right hand of God." (NASB)

There are many of us, including her family, who believe that Stephanie had this same experience when she looked into the corner of that hospital room. And just like Stephen, she fell asleep. I have known Stephanie's family for a long time. They are real people just like all of us. I watched them walk through this horrible situation and I have watched them deal with life on this side of that horrible situation. If ever I have known a family that could have felt like they were "just outside of hope" on multiple occasions, it would certainly be this family. I wonder during all those hospital stays, surgeries, and treatments, if the temptation was not to just give up and say this is hopeless? And how do you deal with this kind of loss?

The words of Stephanie's mom speak volumes:

"A week later God gave me the rest of the story in Isaiah 54. It says 'O afflicted one, storm tossed and troubled; I will rebuild you on a foundation of sapphires and make the walls of your house from precious jewels.' It will not surprise you to know that sapphires were Stephanie's birthstone. 'In righteousness you will be established, you will be far from oppression, for you will not fear, and from terror, for it will not come near you.' I can tell you as her mother that fear never came near Stephanie even though she was sick for seven long years. My wonderful husband and our other children are still deeply in love with our Savior and grateful for the time He allowed us to spend with Stephanie. The years since her "homecoming" have been hard but we still choose to 'Fix our eyes not on what is seen but on what is unseen.' We look forward to Eternity, for Jesus will be waiting, and so will Stephanie."

CHAPTER 18

A Changed Life

I was a little nervous, but very excited about the opportunity to take some of our medical volunteers into a prison in Eastern Venezuela. I had seen prisons in other parts of the country and they were very depressing with conditions that were more than just a little inhumane. I was concerned about how this experience might affect the two medical doctors and one dentist who were part of the volunteer team from the U.S. A Venezuelan Christian who lived in that city had received permission for us to visit the prisoners and offer them medical and dental services, and the team knew there would be divine appointments awaiting us. It was an open door that we felt we must walk through.

We were met at the entrance to the prison by a group of six men, all prisoners and all Christians. Each of them had received Christ since being placed in this prison and you could see the excitement in their faces about meeting Christians from another country. They formed a circle around us and gave us instructions to stay inside their circle of protection as we walked across the courtyard and through several rooms where large groups of prisoners were housed. They walked us into a large cell and literally slammed the door closed behind us. We were definitely in prison.

The cell door was locked and these men would stand by our side for protection and assistance. And, they would process and filter any patients to be seen by the medical volunteers while enjoying the fellowship of being with other Christians.

It really was quite organized. These six men seemed to have the respect of the other prisoners and they kept things moving orderly and peacefully. The only prisoners allowed in the cell were those being attended to at that moment by the medical doctors and dentist.

I was translating for the dentist and my assistant/protector was a prisoner named Alfredo. During the course of the day, I found myself becoming very attached to him. He was one of the kindest men I had ever met. His instructions to the other prisoners were given in such a gentle, caring tone that their harshness and hardness would be defused almost immediately. Alfredo and I talked together almost constantly for the eight hours we were in the prison. There was only one other translator in the cell with us, so I was called upon at times to talk to some of the men who had spiritual questions. Alfredo never left my side.

Our medical team did an incredible job that day of taking care of medical and dental needs and of sharing the love of the Lord. Many of the men wanted to hear their testimonies and why they would be willing to come into a Venezuelan prison. One of the men was so moved by the testimony of our American dentist, who worked non-stop without a break, that he prayed to receive Christ as his Savior. Our dentist pulled 69 teeth that day. Twenty-one prisoners prayed and gave their hearts and lives to Jesus.

As the day ended and all the patients had been seen, we had a wonderful prayer time with our six protectors, who were now close brothers in Christ. We wept together knowing that we would probably not see each other again until heaven. Alfredo and I held on to each other for a long time as we prayed for each other. It was a very emotional good-bye. It's not that unusual to meet a sweet-spirited, kind, gentle man. However, you might not expect to meet such a man in a Venezuelan prison. The last thing Alfredo said to me before the guards walked us out of the lockup was, "I hope you remember my name."

Before leaving the grounds, we met with the prison officials for coffee and to thank them for giving us permission to visit the prisoners. It dawned on me that I had no idea why Alfredo had been sent to prison. He never offered the information and I never asked him as we visited that day. I asked one of the guards if he could tell me about Alfredo. He told me that Alfredo had killed seven men. He had killed four of those while in prison. The last one had been decapitated and his head had been placed on the guard's desk. The guard continued by saying, "About two years ago, Alfredo became very religious and since then he has been a changed man."

Even in a situation that most would describe as hopeless, Alfredo was always "just outside of hope." I'm thankful that the only Alfredo I know is the one who was radically changed by the power of God's salvation ... the kind, gentle, tender-hearted Alfredo. *"Therefore, if anyone is in Christ, he is a new creature; the old things passed away; behold, new things have come."* (2 Corinthians 5:17 NASB)

CHAPTER 19

The Passion of Prayer

One of the things that seems to happen during mission trips is an increased intensity or increased burden to pray for the lost. There are probably many explanations for this intense desire to pray, but I believe the primary reason is best described simply as God's activity. It is true that the best way to pray for people is to pray for them as you are looking at them, walking in their neighborhoods, or listening to their voice. Some refer to this as "praying on site." When you know something about that person, their circumstances, their spiritual journey, and their degree of receptivity, somehow your prayers become much more personal and crucial.

Our volunteer team had been assigned to a small mission church in eastern Venezuela. The pastor and his wife had made arrangements for us to visit in the neighborhoods during the day and participate in evangelistic services at night. One of the church members had taken off from work without pay to walk with us and escort us through the neighborhoods as we made those visits. God was truly at work that week. We saw many people accept Christ as Savior.

I remember a mother and two daughters who prayed to receive Christ. A pastor's wife, who had never had assurance of salvation, also made a decision for Christ that week. As our teams continued to visit, two sisters living in different houses prayed to trust in Jesus at the same time and met in the street as they ran to share the good news with each other. I remember a 14-year-old girl who accepted Jesus and spent the rest of the day going door to door, telling her friends and neighbors about her "new life."

I remember another 14-year-old girl named Nairovis. In fact, I will never forget her. She was a beautiful young lady who hung out at the church all week long with her twin sister. The pastor could only tell us that she and her sister had just started attending the church. It was obvious from the first time we met these girls that Nairovis was much more interested in the Gospel than her sister. She came to the worship services each night. We would see her during the day as we walked through the neighborhood. I'm not sure why God gave me such a burden for her. Maybe it was because my daughter, Kelly, was about the same age at the time. I prayed for Nairovis all week long and fully expected her to make a decision for Christ each night of the revival when the invitation was extended. She never did. As we came to the last night of the revival, Nairovis was present in the service and it seemed that she was truly under conviction, but the service ended, and she still had not made a public decision.

I left the church that night with a heavy heart. The next day we would be heading to the airport in the afternoon to begin our journey back to the United States. That night I could not sleep because of an incredible desire in my heart to see this young lady accept Christ. It was almost 3 a.m. when I woke up my roommate and asked him if he would join me in prayer for this young girl's salvation. One reason I am sharing this story is because, in all honesty, I had never had such a burden for one individual. I knew something of being burdened for "lost people," but I had never been so profoundly impacted over the salvation of one specific person. I literally could not get this young lady's need for Christ out of my mind.

In those moments, I understood for the first time the words of the Apostle Paul, "... *that I have great sorrow and unceasing grief in my heart. For I could wish that I myself were accursed, separated from Christ for the sake of my brethren* ..." (Romans 9:2-3 NASB). I understood that only the Holy Spirit could give that kind of burden, that kind of intense desire to see someone give their heart to Jesus.

The next morning, I knew that I must talk with Nairovis one more time. I drove to the neighborhood where she lived, found her house, and knocked on the door. Her mother answered the door and I explained to her who I was and asked if I could speak with her daughter in the presence of her and her husband. She invited me into the living room and soon the entire family was present. I spoke to Nairovis as if she were the only person in the room and told her that I could not leave the city without giving her one more opportunity to trust in Christ. I asked her what was keeping her from making this decision. She looked up at me with hopeful eyes and said, "I do not feel I can make this decision without my parents' permission."

Immediately, I turned to her parents and explained the decision that Nairovis desired to make. It was an open invitation to explain the gospel to this family. After a few questions and a clear explanation of how a person prays to receive Christ, the father said, "This is an individual decision and if this is what she wants to do, then she has my permission." I can still see the smile on her face and the light in her eyes as we knelt together in that home and, with her parents' permission and in their presence, this 14-year-old girl asked Jesus to forgive her of her sins and come into her life. Nairovis was the only member of her family who prayed that prayer that day.

I have thought about that family many times since that special day. I do not know why God gave me such a burden for one specific individual. All I know is that He prompted me to pray

and He gave me a burden that could not be ignored or neglected. He would not let go of my heart until that young girl
had one more opportunity to receive Christ. I regret to say
there have been few times in my life I have prayed with that
kind of passion.

CHAPTER 20

Meeting Needs and Sowing Seeds

The 1999 Izmit earthquake occurred on August 17, at 3:01 a.m. local time in northwestern Turkey. The shock had a magnitude of 7.6 and lasted for 37 seconds, killing around 20,000 people and leaving more than 250,000 people homeless. On October 8, 1999, we took our first volunteer team into Turkey to assist with humanitarian needs, to work alongside other believers, and to seek opportunities to share the Gospel. At the time, Turkey had a population of 60 million with only one-tenth of 1 percent being Christians. However, over the next few years, we would make seven trips into this Muslim nation and each trip would provide many opportunities to plant, water, and cultivate the seeds of the Gospel. We found the majority of Turkish people to be very warm, friendly, and open for conversations.

Our first visit gave us a close-up view of the devastation caused by the earthquake. Tall apartment buildings were "pancaked" into rubble. Since the quake occurred while people were sleeping, many never had the chance to escape the crumbling buildings. Those who did survive had to wait until sunrise to look for survivors and to see the extent of the damage. We were told that loud wailing could be heard above the sound of machinery being used in the search and recovery attempts. Families stood huddled together over piles of rubble where uncovered bodies of loved ones remained. We heard stories of people jumping out of third- and fourth-story apartments to find, to their amazement, that their apartments were now at ground level.

Amid all the tragic stories, there were also miraculous stories of rescue and stories of "a man dressed in white," who brought water to some who were trapped and waiting to be rescued. I would hear stories about "the man dressed in white" for the next 10 years as I traveled to six different Muslim nations. It seems that even those who appear to be in extreme darkness and distress are "just outside of hope."

In several different locations, prefab units had been set up for those whose homes had been destroyed. It was estimated that it would take at least two years to rebuild permanent structures, so these temporary locations would become a place for survivors to also rebuild their lives. Community centers were placed in each location and these centers became platforms for ministry. Day care for children, English classes, computer classes, and job training for women were all identified as priority needs, as well as opportunities to build relationships. Many women living in these temporary units had lost their husbands and other male family members. Their futures were uncertain without a way to support themselves.

During our many trips to Turkey, we would prayer walk in eight different cities, drink dozens and dozens of glasses of hot tea, drink gallons of a yogurt drink called, Ayran (which I hope we have in heaven), have delicious meals in Turkish homes with families we had just met, be invited to share our stories in schools, give away hundreds of "gifts," which contained New Testaments and DVDs of the Jesus film, have spiritual conversations in homes, in shops, and with taxi drivers.

Some of those conversations were with Imams from local mosques, who were intrigued by our presence in their neighborhoods. In one city the local police escorted us out of town, fearful for our safety. They explained that we were in a very "conservative part of the city and some were angry." However, the police officers asked for a few of our "packages" before leading us out of town. It is impossible to relate all of the incredible experiences we had in our many visits to Turkey, but a few have become spiritual markers in my life.

His name (not his real name) was Amet. He was 10 years old, living in an orphanage for boys in Istanbul. We met during my first visit in 1999 and we were immediately drawn to each other. For the next several years, each time I returned to Turkey I would plan a visit to the orphanage. I would always take a small gift and he would always respond with his signature half smile. I love that smile.

Those in charge of the orphanage told me that Amet's father was serving life in prison for murdering the boy's mother. He had no other family members who stepped forward to take care of him. Christian friends living in Istanbul were faithful to visit the boys in that orphanage and I was happy to learn that Amet had expressed interest in hearing more of the stories from the New Testament. I was told that when he turned 18 years old, he would be enlisted in the Turkish army. I have no idea where he is today or what kind of life he may be living. I know that the seed of the Gospel has been sown in his heart and I pray that I will see him in heaven. I think about him often and God reminds me that even a boy in a Turkish orphanage located in a nation of 60 million and a city of 15 million is "just outside of hope."

Although I knew Amet by name, I'll probably never know the name of the girl with the haunting eyes. I first saw her during our second visit to the earthquake areas. We were involved in food distribution and prayer walking in a city that, before the earthquake had a population of 800,000. Since the quake, most people had left the area, leaving a population of 200,000.

As we walked the streets praying, my eyes were drawn to this young Muslim woman, who was completely covered in her black burka. The only thing not covered was her eyes. Her haunting eyes told a hundred stories. I would guess her to be no older than 20, but her eyes were filled with fear, panic, uncertainty, and desperation. I watched her make her way hurriedly down the street as I prayed for her to seek and find the Truth someday, somehow, somewhere. A friend with whom I was prayer walking said, "Stan, has it dawned on you that we could be the first people who ever specifically prayed for these people?" That thought has forever changed the way I pray for specific people.

Only a few streets over, I saw the young girl with the haunting eyes again and this time, believing that God had allowed me to see her a second time for a purpose, I prayed with much more passion and fervor for her to see "the man dressed in white." Toward the end of the day, she appeared again. Three times God had allowed me to catch a glimpse of this young girl in a busy city filled with shoppers.

Twenty years later I can still picture those eyes and see the fear and uncertainty. I know that God allowed me to pray specifically for her three times that day. I know that God often speaks to Muslim culture through dreams and visions. I know that "the man dressed in white" has identified himself to many Muslims as Jesus, the Son of God. I hope to see that young lady in heaven one day with clear, smiling eyes, and I hope to see her peaceful face because the last time I saw her she was "just outside of hope."

One other God-ordained Turkey experience that is a spiritual marker occurred during our third visit in May 2000. The community centers were open, and we were asked to set up a sewing center for many of the widows. We traveled to Istanbul and made it through customs with 10 electric sewing machines, tables for sewing, and $400 worth of electric converters. I stayed in a 40-foot by 10-foot metal container. The three ladies traveling with me stayed in a similar container, but mine was the only one with hot water. These "Container Hilton's" were equipped with electric heaters and bunk beds and were located close to a community center. While these ladies worked each day with the sewing ministry, I was free to prayer walk and run errands, like trying to find glue in a city without transportation. Having no ability to speak Turkish was another major issue.

Just over the hill were hundreds of prefab dwellings and thousands of homeless people. There was also a mosque overlooking the dwellings and just beside the mosque was a great place to stand and pray. My prayer-walking friend from our last trip showed up in a rental van and we decided to add "prayer driving" to our list of experiences. We prayed for God's direction for the day, where to go and what to do. We drove to the waterfront where the sea had reclaimed about 25 meters of the city weeks after the earthquake. We parked the van to walk the streets, and as I got out of the vehicle, a Turkish man approached me and said, "Are you American? Are you Christian?" He invited us to sit with him and two of his friends and have tea. As we sat on stools outside his shop, we attempted to communicate through gestures and a Turkish dictionary.

My friend had been in this city immediately following the earthquake and had personally worked in the relief camp sponsored by a local automobile assembly plant. These men thought we were asking directions to the assembly plant so they jumped into their car and motioned for us to follow. With great uncertainty and much prayer, we followed these men for about 20 minutes until we arrived at the security gate of the plant where our guides waved to us as they sped away, leaving us in the care of a large security guard who spoke no English. He showed us where to park the van and personally led us through several buildings until we arrived at a large office, where several men were meeting around a large oval table. The security guard motioned for us to sit, and we remained silent as the men continued their meeting. Someone brought us more tea as we waited for the meeting to end or for someone to acknowledge our presence.

Finally, the man at the head of the table, who was the CEO of the assembly plant, addressed us in perfect English. He asked three questions, "Are you Americans? Are you Protestants? Are you Baptist?" He remembered the presence and commitment of volunteers with Texas Baptist Men during the initial relief efforts. We asked him if there were still areas of the city where food distribution was needed. (As we were following our guides en route to the plant, my friend and I decided that when we were questioned, for our own protection and to seize an opportunity to meet a glaring need, our response should be that we had money for food distribution. I had $700 that a church member had given with these instructions, "You will know when and how to use this.")

The question finally came, "What are you doing here?" We responded with our desire to provide food for those severely impacted. The CEO immediately picked up the phone and called the mayor of the city. He told the mayor that he was sending his assistant over with two Protestant, Baptist, Americans who wanted to buy food for needy people.

When we arrived at the mayor's office, we were served more tea until a translator could be found. We then explained our desire to provide food for the neediest area of the city. The mayor listened intensely, opened the middle drawer of his large desk, and pulled out a tall stack of papers and dropped them forcefully on the top of his desk. The young lady serving as our translator leaned over and said in a low voice, "He is saying that these papers are from Muslim organizations and Muslim nations who have promised to send help and none of them had followed through, but these two men walk into my office off the street willing to help." He called for one of his assistants to accompany us to a distribution store and assist us in buying the right kind of food for Turkish families.

The store was a small, family-owned corner grocery store in the middle of an older neighborhood. The husband and wife owners helped us decide what needed to be included in each food sack and it was determined that we had enough money to provide food for 30 homes. The rental van was so packed with food that the mayor's assistant had to ride in another car as we followed them back to the office.

Arriving there, we were led to another office and introduced to another assistant, who took plenty of time looking over a long list, and, very meticulously, selecting the 30 homes that we would be visiting. As we were waiting, of course we were served more tea. As we left the mayor's office and began our food distribution tour, I commented to my prayer-driving friend that the cynical side of me wondered if we would be delivering food to the mayor's cronies. My friend reminded me that we had asked God to direct our day and we were exactly where God had directed us. He was right and I could not have been more wrong with my cynicism.

We followed the assistant all over town, stopping at his selected homes, and at each stop he explained the circumstances of the home. After the third or fourth stop, it became obvious that he was taking us to the homes of widows. Some were young women, but most were elderly, and all of them had lost husbands and other male family members in the earthquake. We asked and were given permission to pray for the women in the name of Jesus. One elderly lady, who had lost six male family members, wept openly as she ran into the house and brought us a sack of nuts she had been eating from a tree in her back yard. Most of the women were very emotional and all of them were thankful for the food and the prayer.

After the last sack of food had been delivered, our guide jumped into our van and gave us a tour of the most devastated part of the city. Interestingly, it was at the waterfront where our prayer drive had begun that morning. As we drove away from the mayor's office for the last time, our van was empty, but our hearts were full. My friend pulled over to the side of the road and we wept as we prayed. We both agreed that had Jesus personally visited that city on that day, He would have visited those same 30 homes that He had allowed us to visit.

It was then that my friend said to me, "Stan, I tried to rent an economy car, but the van was all that was available. God knew that the van would hold the right amount of food."

In Turkey, I learned once again that there is no such thing as hopeless, that in reality, there are many desperate, panicked, frightened, confused, misled, abandoned, and lonely people who are "just outside of hope."

CHAPTER 21

The Big Country

My first trip to China was in September 2001, almost three weeks after the 9-11 attack on the Twin Towers. Needless to say, there were not that many people on the flight. It was a Discovery Trip to learn about possible ministry opportunities in a particular province. This province had been open to foreigners for only 12 years, so we were given extremely specific instructions about security.

As soon as we checked into our hotel, we received a visit from maintenance, making sure our intercom was working properly in order "for us to be able to hear the music clearly." A few years later we would be back with another group staying in the same hotel. One of our team members was getting dressed and preparing to leave for the day when she mentioned to her roommate that she needed to do some laundry. Almost immediately there was a knock on their door and a hotel employee yelling, "Laundry!" There are many similar stories, but the point is that we were warned to be very careful with our conversations. Of course, the real concern was not for us, but for the believers with whom we would be working. Over the next several years, we would return to this area six times and each visit provided plenty of Divine appointments, new friendships, and opportunities to both encourage and learn from some of the most committed Christians anywhere in the world.

The city we worked in had a population of 1.5 million, but there are 150 cities in China with a population of over one million. It is hard for most of us to comprehend that there are 1.3 billion people in China and most of them are "just outside of hope." It is a fair estimate that there are one billion Chinese who do not have a personal relationship with Jesus. It is also fair to say that what has happened in China in the last 20 years is the greatest movement of the Gospel that has ever taken place anywhere in history. This has not happened without great sacrifice nor without great anointing of Spirit-filled Chinese believers. One of the things that constantly amazed me was the maturity and spiritual discernment of these first-generation believers. I'm convinced that because of the threat of persecution and the obvious spiritual oppression, God has placed Chinese believers on a "fast-track" of spiritual growth.

In my first meeting with house church leaders, I asked them to explain how their small group Bible studies were conducted. One member spoke up, "We read a passage and we ask each person, 'What does this mean to you?' And then we ask the Holy Spirit to tell us what it means." Many times, during my visits there, I would ask my trusted translator a question and her response would be, "We must ask the Holy Spirit."

Our teams were involved in many different types of ministries, including medical clinics (with the approval and careful supervision of the Minister of Health), training of teachers in a private school, English as a Second Language classes, and leadership training of house church leaders. A lot of time was spent prayer-walking the city and the university, which had about 10,000 students. Because of our North American friends who lived there and their strong testimony and faithful praying, we always had opportunities to talk with people about Christ ... we just could not discuss it once we returned to our hotel rooms.

Each time I visited I was blessed to have Sara (not her real name) as my translator. She was a student at the university, extremely intelligent, extremely street smart, and extremely mature in her walk with Christ, even though she was a relatively new Christian. Neither of her parents believed and they were unaware of her decision to give her life to Christ.

She was greatly respected among the house church network in the city. On one of my visits, she accompanied me to nine different meetings for house church leaders. Each meeting lasted for two-three hours and each group study was different, depending on the needs of the group. There were times when Sara would lean over and say to me, "Use your Mark 9 passage," or "This would be a good time for John 11." She was always right.

In one of the meetings, two people were invited who were not Christians. During the discussion, one of the young ladies asked why her life had been so hard. We talked about the words of Jesus, "My yoke is easy, and My burden is light," explaining what it meant to be "yoked" to Christ. She placed her hand to her throat and held up her hand, indicating that she wanted me to stop. Sara said, "You can stop. She says she wants to pray." At this point both non-Christians were led by Sara in a prayer to receive Christ. Another believer took those two new believers into another room and began the process of discipleship.

One of the most humbling experiences was the times of worship with these young leaders. Many times, meeting places would be changed for security reasons. When our meetings were in apartment complexes, there was concern that neighbors might be listening. But that did not stop them from "whisper singing" their praises to God.

One morning Sara informed me that one of her friends wanted to meet a pastor and that she had several work associates who also were interested in meeting a pastor. No one in her group had ever met a pastor. I agreed and we grabbed a taxi and headed for the meeting. When I entered the room, there were 20 ladies waiting … all dressed in pink. As it turns out, Mary Kay cosmetics are very popular in China.

I was a little surprised, but they were even more surprised. They were expecting a bearded man wearing a robe and a tall, pointed hat. That was their impression of a pastor, not someone wearing jeans, Nikes, and carrying a backpack.

Sara suggested that we allow them to ask questions. The first question was, "Who is God?" Honestly, I did not do well with that one. The next question was, "What is church?" We discussed this one for the remaining part of our time and then Sara shared the plan of salvation. Seven of those ladies prayed to receive Christ that night.

There were always stories in each of my six visits to China — stories of those who heard the truth of the Gospel and immediately responded and others who had never heard of Jesus but listened intently. I remember a nine-year-old girl who attended the school where our team was working. After hearing about Jesus on the first day, she brought a gift and asked us to give it to Jesus. At the end of the week, she said that she would keep the gift and give it to Him when she went to heaven.

I will never forget the days we spent in remote mountainous villages of minority groups. We were able to take the Jesus film into one of those villages and we were welcomed warmly and shed tears together when it was time to say goodbye. "Just outside of hope" may seem like too far to travel, but the Gospel finds a way and penetrates hearts and cultures because God is already at work there. I have never experienced anything like the spread of the Gospel in China and I've never met anyone, anywhere like Sara.

CHAPTER 22

Sara's Testimony

"I grew up in a typical Chinese family where I had been taught there is no God and spiritual things are not real, that you only have yourself to believe in. My parents, like lots of typical Chinese parents didn't know how to express their love to me. In our culture, we are very conservative about showing love publicly. Even through today, I have never seen my parents hold hands.

"When I was growing up, my parents thought that I was an easy, stress-free child without much work needed. The truth is that I wasn't that good, but I just knew how to please them. While externally I looked like a very obedient child, inside I had many bad thoughts and I knew how rebellious I was.

"When I was a child my parents were addicted to gambling in a Chinese game called Mahjong. They spent most of their time and energy outside of work playing this game. When I was a child and finished school each day, I had to go to my grandma's home or go home by myself since my parents were gambling. Either I had to fix food for myself or go to the Mahjong place and do homework there and wait for them to finish playing, and then I would go home to sleep. While I knew my parents loved me, I wanted more than the way they expressed their love to me.

"During my second year of college I started going to an optional English class taught by Americans three nights a week. On Wednesday nights you could practice your spoken English during a free talk time. Each Wednesday there was a student who would come to that class and she would talk to me. Immediately, she started sharing Jesus with me in Chinese. Since I didn't want to offend her and didn't know how to set boundaries, I could not help but to listen to her. While Jesus sounded like a western thing to me, this girl kept coming each week and would always directly come to me and talk to me about Jesus. Even though inside I felt this was supposed to be a time to practice English, because I didn't want to be rude, I listened to her. That is how I heard the Gospel over a period of time.

"At the end of the semester we were invited to the American teacher's wedding anniversary. They invited all the students and I was excited to attend this type of party. Once I got there, I realized that this party was so different than parties that I experienced. I was used to parties where people played Mahjong or watched TV. Instead, I saw there were a lot of people singing and people surrounded this couple and laid hands on them and started praying for them. Actually, back then I didn't know this was prayer, but I knew they were saying blessings over them. After this, they stood on the stage and they started to renew their wedding promises to each other to continue to love each other unconditionally.

"When I heard that, I just knew that this was the love, the pure love that I was looking for. I was so amazed that I even verbalized, 'How could they possibly do that?' Believe it or not there was a lady right next to me who heard me, and she started to pull me aside and she asked me a question. 'Do you know why? Because it's Christ love and His love is unconditional. That is how they can love each other like Jesus.' She shared with me one more time who Christ is and what He did for me. I knew I was a sinner in my heart, and I knew that I desired that type of love from Christ. He actually died on the cross for me, so who can do better than that for me?

"The Holy Spirit touched me that night and I knew that I needed to receive Christ as my Lord, so I prayed to believe in Jesus that night. The very next day I started one-on-one discipleship class and started to read the Bible and started to know Jesus.

"I wanted to say thank you to the girl who shared with me regularly about Jesus in that English class. I can clearly remember what she looked like with glasses and her appearance. However, since the time I prayed I never ran into her again. I can't even remember her name, but I believe it may have been God's angel for me to know Him. I believe God used this angel to bring me to know Him." *Hebrews 1:14 "Are not all angels ministering spirits sent to serve those who will inherit salvation?"*

Note: There were very few Christians attending this university and none of them knew this "teacher" or remember seeing anyone with her description on campus.

CHAPTER 23

The Boxing Day Tsunami

The 2004 Indian Ocean earthquake occurred December 26, with an epicenter off west coast of northern Sumatra. It was an undersea megathrust earthquake that registered a magnitude of 9.1 on the Richter Scale. Total damages were $15 billion as a series of large tsunamis up to 100 feet high were created by the underwater seismic activity. Communities along the surrounding coasts of the Indian Ocean were seriously affected, and the tsunamis killed an estimated 227,898 people in 14 countries. The earthquake was one of the deadliest natural disasters in recorded history. The earthquake was the third largest ever recorded. The plight of the affected people and countries prompted a worldwide humanitarian response, with donations totaling more than $14 billion.

One month after this tragedy, I was part of a small group of men to arrive in one of the smaller countries that had been affected by the tsunami. This country had made it known that they wanted no outside help. The reason for their refusal of assistance, even assistance from the United Nations, was that their nation was 100 percent Muslim and "foreigners" were not allowed to visit the parts of the nation that had been most severely impacted. Even though there had been 84 confirmed deaths and 24 citizens were still missing; even though rising water from the quake had measured three-and-a-half feet in some of their homes; even though the primary means of income (fishing) had been devastated as equipment was damaged or lost with the flooding; and even though many had been emotionally traumatized as they watched their homes being flooded and their personal belongings washed out to sea, the national government was still declaring, "We want no outside help."

But some of the citizens had grown weary of having no water, no place to sleep, no schools for their children, and no income or equipment with which to provide for their families. God sent our team at exactly the right time to exactly the right areas of a country that was "just outside of hope."

Two of the men on our team had contacts in South Asia who arranged meetings in three different communities where "foreigners" were not allowed to visit. We divided into three groups, prayed, and headed to our different locations where we would ask for permission to meet with community leaders.

Our team arrived at our destination after a one-and-a half-hour boat ride. We were greeted at the boat dock and questioned. We explained that we were "followers of Jesus" from the United States, that we had seen reports of the devastation on television, that we believed that Jesus had asked us to come and help, and that we had money to assist their community. After receiving permission, we were taken immediately to a meeting, which lasted at least three hours.

The chief (much like a mayor) of the community was very tense as we discussed the priority needs of the 1,500 people living there. He reminded everyone that government permission had to be granted before we could proceed with any assistance. As phone calls were made, it was determined that the primary need was immediate drinking water. The storage tanks, which contained captured rainwater and water from the desalination boats, had been completely destroyed by the flooding. We offered to finance a project that included the purchase and installation of five 2,500-liter water storage tanks. The men of the community would do the installation labor. All materials had to be purchased in the capital city and shipped by boat.

Permission was granted by the government to fund the project by saying the community football (soccer) team was responsible for donating the money. It was reported that the football team also purchased mattresses for the community, computers for the school, and six months of salary for the teachers to enable the 320 students to return to classes.

By noon the next day, all materials had arrived, and work was underway. The five sites chosen for the new water tanks were the two mosques, the school, the government office, and the Health Center. We never met the members of the much-loved football team.

We were allowed to stay in the community as the work was being done. We were comfortable, well fed, and greeted cordially. Over the next few days, I had the opportunity to visit other communities in the country and the reception was the same. We purchased more mattresses and more school equipment for another community. Each time we were introduced to new communities, we would always say, "We are followers of Jesus from the U.S. We saw reports of the devastation on television, and we believe that Jesus wanted us to come."

We had been in country for one week when my cell phone rang at 11 p.m. The man on the phone identified himself as the head of the National Security Service. He asked many questions about what we were doing and how we had received permission to do it. He asked for all names and all locations where we were doing projects. I answered all the questions because I was quite sure that he already had all this information. He thanked me for my cooperation and ended the phone call.

The next morning, I headed back to the capital city (by boat) and met the National Harbor Patrol Boat headed to our community. My phone rang and news had reached our team members that the president of the country was on his way with reporters. Immediately I received another call that our team in another community had met with police on three occasions the night before, but were finally given official permission to continue their work. The result of the president's visit was seen that evening on national television as the government took credit for everything that was being done in the communities we had visited.

We visited this country a total of three times in the year after the tsunami. It would be impossible to mention all the contacts, conversations, and divine appointments we experienced. There were conversations with some citizens who had experienced dreams of a prophet dressed in white with a glowing face. This is a frequent experience in Muslim communities where God is at work. A few copies of the Gospel of Luke (which had been recently translated into the local language) were offered as gifts and accepted.

On our second and third trips there were secret discipleship/training sessions for new believers. There was a baptism and the Lord's Supper was observed in a late-night meeting in the middle of a garden. During that Lord's Supper, speaking through a translator, I explained to seven new Christians, all men, the significance of the cross. It was new information for them and I was careful to explain in detail the cruelty of Roman crucifixion. One of the men stopped me and asked, "What kept him on the cross?" I explained again how the Romans had perfected crucifixion. How the large nails were placed in his hands and feet. He said, "I mean what was it that kept him from using his power to get down off the cross?" I replied that it was the love of God that placed him there and the love of God that kept him there. The man bowed his head, closed his eyes, and shook his head from side to side as he grasped the depth of God's love. I don't think I had ever understood the power of God's love so clearly.

In preparation for the Lord's Supper, we had purchased one bottle of a strawberry drink and one glass. When it was time to "take the cup," one of our team members poured a small amount into the glass, drank it, and handed it to the person seated next to him. Each person poured from the bottle into the glass and drank. The symbolism of each person pouring out the symbolic shed blood was powerful. It was a beautiful demonstration of His dying for each person individually, shedding His blood for individuals. After the service we hugged, cried, and slipped silently out of the garden. It was a moment I will never forget.

There were other moments when eyes were opened to the truth about Jesus. One man exclaimed, "God stopped Abraham from taking the life of his son, but He did not stop Himself!" On more than one occasion we were asked, "Why has no one ever told us this about Jesus?" One man after praying to trust in Jesus said, "I understand that when you transfer trust to Jesus, you can never transfer back."

During one of our three-hour discipleship sessions, I was teaching from John 13:5: *Then He poured water into the basin, and began to wash the disciple's feet and to wipe them with the towel with which He was girded.* As I explained the significance of Jesus taking the towel of a servant and kneeling to wash feet, it occurred to me that I should demonstrate His action. However, we were meeting in a vacant room with no running water and no furniture other than the 5 chairs in which we were seated. I grabbed my bottled water from the backpack and reached for the handkerchief in my back pocket. I knelt in front of one of the men and reached down to take his foot. In that moment, it dawned on me that Muslim culture looks upon the bottom of feet as something very offensive. We were warned not to even cross our legs in a way that would show the bottom of our shoes. It was a sign of disrespect.

As I touched his foot, he withdrew and threw up his hand as if to say," Stop!" I said to him, "That's exactly what Peter did!" I read verse 6: "*So, He came to Simon Peter. He said to Him, 'Lord, do you wash my feet?'*" (NASB) As I read the remaining part of the passage, explaining that Jesus was revealing His heart and the heart those disciples must have to carry on His ministry, he put down his hand and lowered his foot. Using the bottled water and the handkerchief I washed the feet of those new believers. Afterwards one of the men, referring to the servant-hearted attitude of Jesus, said, "This kind of love is the only hope for our country."

Later, the same man asked me this question: "If to lie is a sin, is it a sin to lie if I know that to tell the truth would result in my death?" I had no answer. I could only read him these verses from Matthew 10:16-20: "*Behold, I send you out as sheep in the midst of wolves; so be shrewd as serpents and innocent as doves. But beware of men, for they will hand you over to the courts and scourge you in their synagogues; and you will even be brought before governors and kings for My sake, as a testimony to them and to the Gentiles. But when they hand you over, do not worry about how or what you are to say; for it will be given you in that hour what you are to say. For it is not you who speak, but it is the Spirit of your Father who speaks in you.*" (NASB) The country is located in South Asia. In that part of the world there are 1.5 billion people who are "just outside of hope." Each day 30,000 people die in that part of the world without a personal relationship with Jesus … those are tsunami-like proportions that are never called to our attention. Pray for the brothers and sisters in Christ in that part of the world. They have the hope that others need and they risk their lives to share it with those who are "just outside of hope."

CHAPTER 24

Karachi Krazy

My first trip to Karachi, Pakistan, was a Discovery/ Discernment visit to answer two questions: (1) Was it safe enough to take volunteers? (2) Were there opportunities for long-term Christian ministry? The answer to No. 2 was a definite "Yes." The answer to number 1 led me to confirm the belief I had always held that missions volunteers must have a clear calling to participate in a project. It is that confirmation of calling that provides peace regardless of circumstances.

Is Karachi, Pakistan, a safe place for North American Christians to go? Probably not — at least not without a sense of calling and a clear understanding of certain dangers and how best to avoid them. I have participated in over 50 international missions trips and the only time I ever felt fear was in Pakistan.

One of the first men I talked to on the street said to me, "I am very surprised that you came here; it is very risky." My journal entry after our second day in Karachi read, "There is darkness and danger here — also, He is at work here. I must trust Him for every step and must be filled with the Holy Spirit in order to interpret His promptings. Prayers for a necessary boldness as well as discernment."

There are many followers of Jesus in Pakistan. There are a few Christian churches there. There are many miraculous stories of those who were "just outside of hope" and were brought to the Truth of the Gospel through the power of God.

The first Christian I met there was a young lady working in a bookstore. I was introduced to her by friends who told me that I must hear her story. I was the only customer in the store, but we stood near the back between rows of books and she spoke in a low voice. She was from a large Muslim family (five brothers and five sisters) in the northern part of the country. As a child, she was very respectful of her family and their conservative Muslim beliefs and practices. She prayed five times a day as she had been instructed, but since the age of nine or ten, and without her family's knowledge, she had always ended her prayers by saying silently, "If this is not the truth, show me the truth."

When she was 14, while in her bedroom, she prayed that silent prayer and immediately the room filled with light. She explained that it was a very bright light or a vision of a light and it was "turning around and around." She then heard a voice coming from the light, repeating the same words in her language until she was able to write them down. When she had written those words, the light disappeared and she read the words over and over to herself. She hid the piece of paper on which she had written the words and pondered their meaning for months. She could think of no one in her town, and certainly no one in her family, with whom she might share those special words or who might explain their meaning. As she kept her secret, she continued to pray that silent prayer, "… show me the truth." I'm not sure how much time elapsed before she heard about an elderly Christian woman living in a nearby town. She secretly traveled by bus to that town and met the Christian woman. She showed the woman the piece of paper, which contained the words she had heard. The woman opened a Bible (something the teenage girl had never seen) and began to search and read the pages as if she expected to find those words. After several minutes, she pointed to the words found in Isaiah 48:16-17 — "*Come near to Me, listen to this: From the first I have not spoken in secret, From the time it took place, I was there. And now the Lord GOD has sent Me, and His Spirit." Thus says the LORD, your Redeemer, the Holy One of Israel, "I am the LORD your God, who teaches you to profit, Who leads you in the way you should go."* (NASB)

Those were the exact words the girl had heard and recorded on her piece of paper. That day she became a follower of Jesus. She kept her commitment to Christ a secret for as long as she could, but her family soon began to notice changes in her attitude toward her Muslim traditions. One of her uncles approached her privately and told her that if she had converted to Christianity that she should flee to a large city, like Karachi, or her family would be obligated to kill her. She took his warning seriously and here she was in a city of 15 million people, working in a bookstore.

One of our contacts in Pakistan was a man in whom we had great confidence and trust. He had years of experience living in Muslim culture and talking with Muslims about the teachings of the New Testament. In order to better understand both the culture and Muslim teachings, he suggested that we go to a local mosque and have a conversation with the Lead Teacher (Imam). We found a taxi driver who was willing to take us to the nearest mosque, but we were not allowed to enter. In fact, we went to several mosques, but were turned away. At one, our driver was approached and asked, "Why did you bring these men here?"

We were finally directed to the main Teaching Mosque, which was described as something similar to a "Seminary for Imams." We were welcomed and told, "Our book says that we must welcome anyone who comes seeking answers to questions." We were asked to remove our shoes and to be seated on the floor with the Imam and other teachers. I guessed there to be 20-25 men seated on the floor around us. We were served hot tea and everyone was extremely courteous ... and curious.

Our leader immediately began to mention passages in their book that referred to Jesus and I sensed that the men were impressed with his familiarity with the book, but also suspicious of that familiarity. The Imam became a little uncomfortable with some of the teachings about Jesus that were contained in their book, but obviously never emphasized. The men in the group grew more and more interested as my friend pointed to verses that told of Jesus performing miracles, healing the sick, raising the dead, and knowing the way to the Father.

At that point I noticed the man seated beside me was leaning forward with his hand cupped behind his ear, straining to hear every word that was being spoken. Our conversation lasted for over two hours, but ended abruptly when the Imam asked for proof that Joseph was not the father of Jesus. When we showed him Matthew 1:18-25 in his own Ingil (New Testament), he told us we had stayed long enough and encouraged us to continue to seek the truth.

I can still picture that man seated to my right as he leaned forward straining to hear what was being said about Jesus. I believe that he was seeking truth and I believe him to be a picture of many in the Muslim world who are closer and closer to faith in Jesus.

We continued to take small teams of volunteers to Pakistan over the next few years. The Lord provided several unique ministry opportunities and many open doors and influential contacts in different parts of the city, but as one team member accurately explained, "We always had one hand tied behind our back." There was always opposition.

We were providing a medical clinic in one part of the city and things were going well. We had seen over 200 patients when the police arrived and told us we had 10 minutes to get out of the neighborhood. A terrorist had been killed blocks away and his followers were protesting. We packed up in record time and received a police escort back to our hotel.

The next day we were in another part of town and once again our medical clinic was attending to the needs of hundreds of people. But, there were threatened protests nearby and the people feared for our safety. Once again, we had to close the clinic earlier than planned.

One area of the city housed about 400,000 people who are considered the poorest of the poor. It is one of the most poverty-stricken areas I have ever seen. A contact from that area received permission from the Taliban for us to offer a medical clinic inside one of the local mosques. We arrived and were greeted with the news that the mosque was no longer available because members of Al Qaeda were sleeping at the mosque. We waited as options were discussed and finally permission was given to conduct the clinic in a school. We began to unload equipment and arrange to see patients, when the police arrived to escort us out of the neighborhood. We explained that we had asked and received permission from local "leaders," but the police were insistent. They were very concerned for our safety and were not willing to "risk the lives of so many Americans." The ladies in our group were allowed to leave with our drivers, but some of our drivers were not scheduled to return until later that day. The men in our group were escorted out by heavily armed policemen and placed into the back of two mobile police trucks. We were taken to the police station and kept until our drivers could be located.

At the police station we had a chance to meet the police captain and discuss with him and other policemen about our ministry and our motivation. We were treated well and even received a police escort back to our hotel. We still refer to those events as, "just another typical day in Karachi."

As I mentioned, there are Christians in Pakistan and the challenges they face are extreme, but the Gospel they proclaim is powerful. Even though it is a dark and dangerous place, the millions of people living there are not beyond the reach of the Light. They are "just outside of hope."

114

Note: When I think of Karachi, three images come to mind. The man in the mosque with his hand cupped over his ear, straining to hear the message; the red bearded man driving a white van who tried his best to run over me, but missed by inches: and a 10-year-old girl who had the sweetest face and the dirtiest feet I have ever seen. I am convinced that her feet had never, ever been washed. I will never forget those three images, which represent the search for truth, the danger of heretical teaching, and the innocent victims of that heresy.

CHAPTER 25

Miracle Corner

One of the greatest blessings of my ministry has been the opportunity to take youth groups on mission trips. I believe that every young person would benefit from spending time in another culture, listening to another language, and bonding with people who aren't exactly like them. One of the greatest blessings of being a Christian is to experience unity in diversity. I have seen youth and adults who do not speak the same language and who come from very different backgrounds become lifelong friends after spending a week together. The key element is their unity in Christ. Time and time again I have witnessed this, but nowhere is this more common than in Brazil.

Brazil is a great place to visit because of the openness of the people, the great weather, the great food, and the movement of the Holy Spirit. During our visits to Brazil, we have seen many people make the decision to dedicate their lives to become followers of Jesus Christ. And if that were not thrilling enough, the dozens of youth who accompanied us on these trips saw firsthand what can happen when the Gospel is shared in a receptive area. Unlike many of the "closed" nations where we ministered, South America is wide open when it comes to sharing the truth about Jesus, and this is certainly true in Brazil. Brazil is not unlike other South American countries except for the language (Portugués) and their passion for soccer (fútbol).

We were fortunate enough to have been there during a World Cup game and the experience was unforgettable. No one was watching the game in their houses: chairs, sofas, and televisions were brought out into the streets, which were packed with fans passionately cheering for their team. You have never seen soccer until you have watched a World Cup match with a Brazilian!

Another thing Brazil has in common with other South American countries is poverty. In Spanish-speaking countries, they are called "barrios," in Brazil they are called "favelas," but except for the language being spoken, they are the same. Overcrowded settlements of human beings, who are daily struggling to survive in challenging living conditions. I have stated before that poverty smells the same anywhere in the world and poverty was evident in many of the areas in which we worked.

The favela where we ministered during three separate missions trips was referred to as "The Swamp" for obvious reasons, especially during the rainy season. In this neighborhood, inhabited by 15,000 people, we were welcomed and able to provide medical and dental clinics, construction projects, children's Bible school, block parties, speaking in local schools, and walking from street to street "telling the story" of the Gospel. This "story" was told hundreds of times during our visits and it was well received by many who were "just outside of hope."

Gabriel was a 16-year-old gang member who, at first, was very suspicious of our presence in his neighborhood. He watched us closely as we interacted with children during the block party and he promised to attend one of the Bible teaching sessions. Gabriel actually attended one of our nightly revival services held in the neighborhood Baptist Church and on that night, he gave his life to Christ. He told us that he approved of what we were doing and asked if we would come back next year or "just show up every four years like the politicians?" This is one of the main reasons our missions' philosophy was to establish partnerships with missionaries and/or local churches so that we could return to the same areas year after year.

Each day we would send a few teams into the favela to "prayer walk "and to "tell the story." The number of teams depended on the number of available translators.

We wanted our youth to have the opportunity to share their own personal stories and to experience firsthand the power of the Gospel as it is explained to receptive people.

As it turned out, we were short on translators so we decided that I should take two young people with me and see if we could communicate in Spanish. I do not speak Portuguese and the two languages are not as similar as some people think; however, on this particular day it did not seem to matter.

Our team had walked several blocks into the neighborhood when we were approached by a young mother carrying her baby boy. It was obvious that she was concerned for the baby as she rushed up to us explaining that the boy had been sick with a fever for days. She asked if we would pray for her child, whose name was Samuel. As we stood in the middle of the street, a crowd began to gather around us as they waited for us to help this child.

We placed our hands on baby Samuel and prayed in English for God to heal him and to use his healing to bring glory to God. By this time an even larger crowd had gathered and I began to tell the story in Spanish, and, to our amazement, it was obvious that the message was being understood. People began to stand in line to receive prayer and to hear the story. After sharing the story with several, I told the youth team members who were with me that it was their turn to share and that I would translate. For over an hour, we stood on the same corner as person after person stood in line to have their opportunity to receive a personal prayer and to hear the story. Samuel's mother came to tell us that his fever was gone and that he was much better. We returned to that same corner throughout the week and dozens of people prayed to receive Christ on "Miracle Corner."

At the end of that first trip to Brazil, we were waiting on our departure flight at the airport when we heard a slight commotion at the entrance. We saw a small group of young men walking in our direction and they were receiving a lot of attention from security and other travelers. We recognized the young man in front of the group … it was Gabriel!! He walked directly up to us and pointed to another young man in his group and said, "This is my brother, Vincent. He wants to hear the story." Vincent was in his early twenties and he and his friends drove to the airport to hear the story that Gabriel had been talking about. Vincent prayed to receive Christ in the airport.

The next year we were right back in the same area with another team. Our first stop after arriving in the favela was to Miracle Corner where we immediately saw three of the ladies who had accepted Christ the year before. We saw Samuel's mother and she was happy to report that he had not been sick at all since our last visit. We asked about Roseanna, whom we had visited in her home and who had AIDS. She had given her heart to Christ during our visit, but we were told that she had passed away soon after our last trip. I believe we will see her in heaven, healed, healthy, and no longer outside of hope.

It is impossible to write about all the wonderful memories and even more impossible to put into human words the supernatural activity of God. There are moments, holy moments, when there is such an obvious presence of God that there is no denying it. Some of those moments are subtle, but just as holy.

As we walked the streets praying, we saw a middle-aged man working in front of his simple house. He was dressed like most men working in the hot sun. He had on a pair of shorts and sandals. We spoke to him and he walked over to greet us by the low fence in front of his house. He was curious about our presence in the neighborhood but was interested in hearing the story. As we explained how the death of Jesus on the cross not only provided forgiveness for our sin, but also made it possible for us to receive eternal life, this man began to have tears in his eyes. He very quickly responded to the invitation to pray and ask Jesus to take control of his life. But before he prayed, he turned, ran into his house, and returned with a shirt. He was not going to pray without putting on a shirt. I don't remember when one small, and some would say insignificant, act touched me so deeply. It was a holy moment created by a man who recognized the significance of what he was about to do. I shall never forget him.

These holy moments can occur anywhere, even in a pizza restaurant.

On one of our Brazil trips, we quickly made friends with our van driver, Rodrigo. He accompanied us all week as we moved from project to project, even sitting in on our nightly Home Group Bible studies. He asked if he could bring his wife, Thatiana, to one of the studies, and during the teaching that night, it was obvious she was very interested.

The study that evening was about Noah and his family and the deliverance and safety they experienced in the Ark. After the study, as we enjoyed pizza at our favorite pizza place, the conversation continued not only about the truth of the passage, but also about the symbolism of the Ark as it reveals God's gift of salvation. It was then that Thatiana revealed that she had recently been diagnosed with cancer. She wanted to know if she could be saved and delivered. Our translator shared the Gospel with Thatiana and with tears flowing, she prayed and asked Jesus to be her Savior. She entered the Ark of salvation in a pizza place.

A few years later she departed this life and entered safely into the arms of her Savior.

The gang member, his brother, Samuel's mother, the young lady with AIDS, the man working in front of his house, the dozens who were touched on Miracle Corner, and the beautiful young lady with cancer, had all been living their lives "just outside of hope." But one day they heard the story and believed it, trusted it, submitted their lives to it, and found the hope of eternal life through faith in Jesus Christ. The story must be told!

CHAPTER 26

Witchcraft, Spiritualism and Demonic Influence

Shortly after our building was in place and weekly services had begun at a new church plant in Venezuela, we started noticing the charred remains of small animals around the building, especially at the front door. Those attending the church explained that the neighborhood "bruja" (witch) was offering sacrifices and praying against the church.

"Brujería," or witchcraft, is very common in most countries in Central and South America. You will find in many neighborhoods a person to whom some will go for potions to cast spells or remove spells, to heal injuries or diseases, or for spiritual instructions concerning the future. The bruja in our neighborhood was obviously not happy about having a Baptist Church less than two blocks from her house. As the church increased in numbers, the "burnt offerings" at the front door soon ceased, but the influence of spiritism in the lives of the people continued to be a stronghold.

One of the young ladies from the neighborhood, Nuris, began attending the church. She was 22 years old, unmarried, and the mother of a baby boy. Others in the church persuaded Nuris to talk to me about an injury just above her ankle that was infected. She was in noticeable pain and was limping as she walked. She had gone to the bruja to receive treatment and the bruja had "blessed" an ankle bracelet and placed it on Nuris' leg just below the infected area. I asked her if she would be willing to remove the ankle bracelet. She responded that she had been trying to remove it for days, but each time she touched the bracelet it would get hot, so hot that she could not touch it and it would begin to burn her leg.

We prayed for her and shared the message of salvation with her. I told her that Jesus had the power to not only remove the bracelet, but also the power to deliver her from the evil influences upon her life. This was not an easy decision for her. She was afraid to tempt the power of the bruja. She was reluctant to reject the traditions and teachings of her family. In her mind, she was in a hopeless situation, but she saw the changes in the lives of her neighbors who had recently come to faith in Jesus Christ. She saw a new hope. She listened to the presentation of the Gospel and she prayed to receive Christ as her Savior. She walked to her house, prayed in the name of Jesus, and quickly removed the bracelet. The next time I saw her, her leg was completely healed, and she became a faithful follower of Jesus.

At my request, Nuris took me to the bruja's house. She introduced me to the woman and her teenage daughter. I told them about our church and our beliefs. They both listened attentively, but when I began to explain about the death, burial, and resurrection of Jesus, the bruja could not remain in the room. She walked out into the back yard and paced back and forth as I continued to talk with her daughter. She never came back into the house until we left, but her teenage daughter prayed to receive Christ that day. The power of the message of Jesus can deliver anyone who is willing to believe and call upon His name.

* * *

In the year 2000, I was privileged to travel to Bolivia with 12 guys, eight of whom were high school basketball players. Of course, the purpose of the trip was to share the Gospel, but the platform was basketball. Our guys were to play several competitive games against Bolivian teams as well as lead basketball clinics for children in the neighborhoods. These young men excelled in the games and the clinics. Some of the games were against semi-pro teams and one game was played against the undefeated Women's National Team. Our guys were not too excited about playing this one until they learned that one of the players was Miss Bolivia. It turned out to be a great thing because at halftime the guys were able to share their personal testimonies and give each player a Bible.

The receptionist at our hotel was a young lady named Erica. Several from our group had given her a translated copy of their personal testimony, which led to many questions and some good conversations. Erica described herself as "a very spiritual person." She talked very openly about the group of which she was a part; in fact, she told us that she was the "spiritual medium" of her group and she would "channel conversations with other spirit beings."

After several long discussions with her, she made a statement that indicated just how desperately she was seeking the Lord and gave evidence that God was at work in her life. She said with all sincerity, "I have always wanted a spirit to come and live in me." Wow! Talk about an open door! She was very open to the Scriptures we shared about Jesus and His words about the promise of the Holy Spirit coming to live in the heart of a true believer. We gave her a New Testament and asked her to not attend her group meeting that night, but instead, to stay home and read the passages we had marked for her. She agreed and in our conversation the next afternoon, she prayed to receive Christ as her personal Savior. The Holy Spirit came to make His abode in the heart of this young lady who had been searching for the Truth. She was "just outside of hope" when the Truth found her.

* * *

My first encounter with a Ouija board was in college during the latter part of the 1960's. Some guy on our floor had purchased it and his room was full of onlookers. I watched for maybe 10 minutes, had a strange feeling about it, left, and went to my room.

Ten years later, I was a Southwestern Seminary student and working as a youth pastor in Fort Worth, Texas, when two teenage girls showed up at our church office. They were crying hysterically, were out of breath from running the three blocks from their house to the church, and told us they had been frightened while "messing around with a Ouija board." We never really figured out all that occurred, but it did involve their asking to speak to someone from the "spirit world."

According to the girls, a necklace one of them was wearing became so hot that it was burning her neck and the girls struggled to get it off. My pastor insisted that we all get on our knees and each of us pray in the name of Jesus for the girls to be forgiven and protected. I can testify that there was an immediate calmness and peacefulness in the room. I feel confident those girls never again played with a Ouija board or played around with a spirit world about which they had no real understanding.

I understand that Ouija boards are sold as "harmless" games and that any "messages" received could possibly be the result of ideomotor movements ... unconscious gestures we make in response to strong ideas or emotions. But I also understand that spiritual warfare is reality that should not be denied or ignored.

The fact is that there exists an organized demonic conspiracy, which has as its purpose the disruption of the will of God and the destruction of the people of God. The Bible refers to this as a spiritual warfare that is taking place in the unseen spiritual realm. Keep in mind that just because it is part of unseen reality does not mean it is not real. The reality is that we have an enemy, Satan, who hates us and will do everything within his power to destroy us, to discourage us from trusting in God, and to disrupt our finding and following of God's will for our lives. I chose to use a Ouija board as an example to illustrate that you cannot "play around" with powers that really do exist in the unseen spiritual realm. The Apostle Paul warns us that all our struggles are not against "flesh and blood." He writes in Ephesians 6:12, *"For our struggle is not against flesh and blood, but against the rulers, against the powers, against the world forces of this darkness, against the spiritual forces of wickedness in the heavenly places."* (NASB)

In 2014, we were in Asunción, Paraguay, with a volunteer team, which consisted mainly of teenagers. This was our second trip to this area so the people in the neighborhood knew who we were and what we were about. I do not remember who approached us; it could have been a family member or a concerned neighbor who came to us and asked for our help. They described a young man who, with a group of friends, had been "playing around" with a Ouija board. During the game, this young man had gone into a trance-like condition and was unresponsive to his friends. Over a week had passed and he was still unable or unwilling to respond to friends or family. The only person he had spoken to was his mother and his only communication with her was uncontrolled cursing.

His mother was asking for us to come and pray for him. I asked the oldest youth on our team to accompany me and we wound our way through the neighborhood until we found the right house. As we sat with him on the front porch of their simple home, he was unresponsive and just stared straight ahead, not making eye contact with anyone. Speaking to him in Spanish, I said, "You are in this condition because Satan desires to destroy you and to keep you from finding God's will for your life. I know you can hear me, and I want you to know that Jesus

126

Christ is the only one who can help you." At that point, I did not try to share any portion of Scripture or any explanation of the Gospel message. I simply asked him if he would say the name of Jesus. "There is power in that name," I said.

For the first time, he turned his eyes toward my face, and I saw fear. He began to try to force the word from his lips and after a few attempts at forming the sound, he was able to whisper the name of Jesus. He kept repeating it over and over again until he could say it clearly and confidently.

After a few minutes, his countenance changed, his eyes were brighter, and he began to speak to his mother. We shared the plan of salvation with him and invited him to attend the worship service that evening. We were thrilled when we saw him walk in the door as the service began.

Your spiritual life is not something with which to play around. It is real and your eternal destiny is at stake. The evil powers and forces of spiritual darkness will lead you away from your only hope. They will lead you as far as you allow, but the powerful name of Jesus can reach those who are "just outside of hope." No matter how far away you are, just begin to say the name of Jesus, the name that is above all names. Your countenance will change and your vision will become clearer.

CHAPTER 27

There Is Always Hope

I was "called to preach" at the First Baptist Church in Hope, Arkansas. I was also privileged to pastor my home church for nine years. It is a beautiful church building, constructed in the late 1940's with the kind of handiwork we do not see anymore and could not afford to duplicate. One interesting thing about the building is that on top of the high steeple is a weathervane. Not a cross or a spire, but a weathervane.

One day my office phone rang, and it was a dear friend who had grown up in Hope and worked at a downtown business. He said, "Stan, I'm sitting here looking out my office window and I just noticed that your church has a weathervane on top of the steeple. Why a weathervane?"

I was too embarrassed to admit to him that I had never noticed that either, but I said to him without hesitating, "It's to remind our community that no matter which way the wind is blowing, God is still God and there is always hope." I have no idea why our predecessors chose to put a weathervane on top of the steeple, but I'm sticking to my explanation.

On another occasion, while studying in that office, I heard the sound of a large 18-wheeler pulling into the parking lot outside my window. First Baptist is located downtown on Main Street, several miles from the Interstate, not the usual route for large trucks. The driver came into the church office and asked to speak to the pastor, and when he sat down in my office, he began to cry. He told me that life just wasn't worth living anymore. He had just heard from his wife that when he made it back home, she would not be there. His being on the road for days at a time had contributed to the destruction of his marriage. He was so distraught as he traveled down the Interstate that he thought of taking his own life. Not only was he thinking about it, he planned it. He said to me, "I had lost the will to live and had given up all hope, and I cried out to God in desperation. Immediately, I saw a sign on the Interstate that said, 'Hope Next Exit'. I took that exit and drove until I found the tallest steeple."

I do not remember his name, but that day God directed him to Hope, Arkansas, where he found hope in what he thought was a hopeless situation. I do not know what direction the wind was blowing that day, but the wind of the Spirit was blowing and directing that truck driver toward hope. He was just outside of Hope, Arkansas, when God led him to the Biblical hope of life in Christ.

CHAPTER 28

The Three H's

hy·poc·ri·sy / *noun:* the practice of claiming to have moral standards or beliefs to which one's own behavior does not conform; pretense.

hate / *verb:* feel intense or passionate dislike for (someone).

hope / *noun:* a feeling of expectation and desire for a certain thing to happen.

I had no idea that this book would start coming together in the year of a global pandemic, and in the year of an historic presidential election. So far, we have not made ourselves proud as a nation with our reactions to either challenge. Regardless of where you stand politically, and regardless of your personal perspective of the pandemic, surely you will agree that we are seeing plenty of hypocrisy, plenty of hate, and not much real hope. As stated in an earlier chapter, "hope" is commonly used to mean a wish: its strength is the strength of the person's desire. But in the Bible, "hope" is the confident expectation of what God has promised and its strength is in His faithfulness.

Biblical hope is our only hope. We cannot just strongly wish that our situation will get better and expect any positive changes. Hope based on anything or anyone other than God and His faithfulness can do nothing to deter hypocrisy or hate.

In my opinion, that is where we, those of the church, have failed. We have failed to share the Gospel in the power of the Holy Spirit and for this we are all guilty.

Our cities, big and small, are void of Spirit-filled followers of Christ, who have the only true remedy to the deadly "H" viruses of hypocrisy, hatred, and false hope. What have we been doing? According to John 15:5, nothing of eternal value. Look it up and read it.

Obviously, this book is not about growing up in a place called Hope, but rather it's about people who thought they were beyond hope, and some who did not know that hope was even a possibility, and yet, their situations were not hopeless. The truth is they were just outside of hope, closer than they ever imagined.

There is no such thing as a hopeless situation. Those of us who claim to be Jesus' disciples must take Spirit-led steps to unleash the supernatural, life-changing, redeeming power of the Truth of the Gospel. That is, always has been, and forever will be our only real hope. Some, in fact many, will deny, reject, and refuse to submit to the Truth of Jesus. That is their choice, but the cure is too lifesaving not to share.

"But what does it say? THE WORD IS NEAR YOU, IN YOUR MOUTH AND IN YOUR HEART — that is, the word of faith which we are preaching, that if you confess with your mouth Jesus as Lord, and believe in your heart that God raised Him from the dead, you will be saved; for with the heart a person believes, resulting in righteousness, and with the mouth he confesses, resulting in salvation. For the Scripture says, 'WHOEVER BELIEVES IN HIM WILL NOT BE DISAPPOINTED.' For there is no distinction between Jew and Greek; for the same Lord is Lord of all, abounding in riches for all who call on Him; for 'WHOEVER WILL CALL ON THE NAME OF THE LORD WILL BE SAVED.' How then will they call on Him in whom they have not believed? How will they believe in Him whom they have not heard? And how

will they hear without a preacher? How will they preach unless they are sent? Just as it is written, 'HOW BEAUTIFUL ARE THE FEET OF THOSE WHO BRING GOOD NEWS OF GOOD THINGS!'" (Romans 10:8-15 NASB)

In 1997, while pastoring in my hometown, I received a message from a lady in her 80's who was facing heart surgery the next day. Her family member stated that "she would like to talk with you," so I headed to the hospital. She was a well-known person in our community, and a very active member of another church. As I have reflected on our conversation, I am convinced that she chose to talk with me because of her longtime friendship with my parents. There was a built-in trust factor. I cannot imagine the amount of courage it took for her to call me, and to share with me that she did not have assurance of her salvation.

She was thinking about the dangers of the surgery she would be facing the next morning, and as she did a kind of spiritual inventory of her life, she came to the conclusion that she did not have a peaceful assurance that if she were to die, she would go to heaven. She described a spiritual commitment she had made as a little girl, but she said, "I have never had a real peace about it." And then she said, "Tell me again how to be saved."

Together we read these verses: *"The one who believes in the Son of God has the testimony in himself; the one who does not believe God has made Him a liar, because he has not believed in the testimony that God has given concerning His Son. And the testimony is this, that God has given us eternal life, and this life is in His Son. He who has the Son has the life; he who does not have the Son of God does not have the life. These things I have written to you who believe in the name of the son of God, so that you may know that you have eternal life. This is the confidence, which we have before Him, that, if we ask anything according to His will, He hears us. And if we know that He hears us in whatever we ask, we know that we have the requests which we have asked from Him."* (1 John 5-10-15 NASB)

She prayed that night for Jesus Christ to save her and to give her assurance of her eternal life. We prayed together that her heart would be filled with God-given peace, that she would rest comfortably, and that God would confirm to her that He had heard and answered her prayer.

Later she would tell me that God's peace had filled that hospital room and that one of her confirmations was that she never experienced any pain after her heart surgery. Some time later, she was diagnosed with cancer and she faced death with a courage and a confidence that came from the knowledge that her heart was filled with the presence of Jesus Christ.

Life on Earth is not forever and sometimes we must have the courage to admit that we are not sure, and then to call upon the name of the Lord for eternal life. God wants us to be sure. I share this story with the prayer that you have assurance of your own salvation, and that you have the assurance and confidence that you will go to heaven when you depart this life. If you have never made the personal decision to invite Jesus to forgive you of your sins and to take control of your life, it could be that God is drawing you to Himself even as you read these words. You are closer than you think you are — just outside of hope — call upon the name of the Lord and you will be saved.

Epilogue

After serving in churches in Texas, Arizona, Oklahoma, Costa Rica, Venezuela, and Arkansas, Charlotte and I retired in Arkadelphia, Arkansas, where we first met and were married in 1969. We are finishing where we started, and we are only 50 miles from my hometown of Hope, Arkansas.

After my mother died, Dad sold the house and the land, saying that it "had served its purpose," and that "it just wasn't the same without her." The house has been moved to another location, the large oak tree in front of the house was struck by lightning and had to be cut down, the woods on the backside of the property were turned into pasture, and even some of the pine trees my dad and I planted in the front yard when I was 10 years old have been removed. He was right. It's not the same.

Even now, however, when I drive by our old home place, I can still envision it the way it was when it was Route 4, Box 304 on Melrose Lane, or as my dad would always say, "just outside of Hope." The Baptist church where I received Christ as my Savior is still located a half-mile up the road, but almost everything else in the "neighborhood" is different.

In the year 2000, I was seated on the podium in a church in St Petersburg, Russia, waiting to preach. I remember saying to myself, "This is a long way from Hope, Arkansas," but then the thought occurred, "but Hope is not that far from me." In that moment, I began to reflect on the goodness of God, the faithfulness of my parents, and the wonderful memories of my childhood. As

I sat there, I became very emotional and the tears began to flow down my face. I was struck with the fact that a person like me, with all my flaws, my mistakes, my rebellion, and my years of disobedience, would be called by God, forgiven, cleansed, and given the privilege of proclaiming the Good News of the Gospel. I am still overwhelmed by that characteristic of God's grace.

Charlotte and I recently learned that we are soon to become great grandparents. In all likelihood, our future generations will never know very much about where I grew up "just outside of Hope," but my prayer is that they will know the hope of abundant life and the hope of eternal life through faith in Jesus Christ.

I don't know what their world might look like, or what they might face in the future, but I want them to know that even in the most desperate moments when, perhaps, they feel a long way from hope, that hope is never far from them.

About the Author

The Rev. Stan Parris is retired as pastor of Second Baptist Church in Arkadelphia, Arkansas, a small town that is home to two universities — Henderson State University, a public school, and Ouachita Baptist University, a private Southern Baptist University school that supplies more denominational preachers and music ministers than any school in Arkansas. Stan graduated from Henderson, which is a small part of the unusual path of his life from "just outside of Hope," Arkansas, where he grew up, to All-American college football player, to an NFL camp where he was one misstep from making the team, to coaching high school football, then surrendering to his long-held call to the ministry, which led to a call to missions.

He graduated from Southwestern Baptist Theological Seminary in Fort Worth, Texas, then pastored churches in Arizona, Oklahoma and Arkansas, became missions pastor at one of the largest Southern Baptist Churches in his home state, eventually ending his fulltime ministry in the town where and when football was No. 1 in his life. His priorities changed, both with his marriage and his call to the ministry. His love of preaching has not diminished in retirement, leading him to interim pastorships and opportunities to fill in for pastors on leave or vacation.

Stan married his college sweetheart, Charlotte Wilson Parris, and they have three children, Kyle, Kelly, and Kenneth. Stan and Charlotte also are "Papa" and "Nana" to five grandchildren — Alexa Nicole, Dustyn James, Sara Elizabeth, Charlee Lane and Campbell Elise.

CPSIA information can be obtained
at www.ICGtesting.com
Printed in the USA
BVHW070603051021
618104BV00002B/4